PANDEMICS AND SPIRITUAL SEEKERS

Many of us are somewhat paralysed by confusion, sadness and anxiety due to the uncertainty and devastating effects caused by the COVID-19 pandemic. Paul Kraus, from the depth of his spirituality, has gathered a rich collection of spiritual writings from various 'saints and sinners' for this book. This volume unequivocally assists us in finding true freedom during this time of crisis and in the way it has affected our lifestyle. I thank Paul for this book and strongly recommend it to anyone yearning for peace at this tumultuous time.

Father Bryan Roe
Parish Priest of St Benedict's Parish
Archdiocese of Brisbane.

LOCATING OUR
INVISIBLE WOUNDS

PANDEMICS AND SPIRITUAL SEEKERS

PAUL KRAUS

Published in Australia by
Coventry Press
33 Scoresby Road
Bayswater VIC 3153

ISBN 9780648982227

Copyright © Paul Kraus 2021

All rights reserved. Other than for the purposes and subject to the conditions prescribed under the *Copyright Act*, no part of this publication may be reproduced, stored in a retrieval system, or transmitted in any form or by any means, electronic, mechanical, photocopying, recording or otherwise, without the prior permission of the publisher.

Scripture quotations are from the *New Revised Standard Version Bible*, copyright 1989, Division of Christian Education of the National Council of the Churches of Christ in the United States of America. Used by permission. All rights reserved.

Catalogue-in-Publication entry is available from the National Library of Australia http://catalogue.nla.gov.au

Cover design by Ian James – www.jgd.com.au
Text design by Coventry Press
Set in Tex Gyre Pagella

Printed in Australia

Table of Contents

A Christian world view 5

Foreword
    Archbishop Mark Coleridge 6

Introduction
    Paul Kraus 8

Part 1   The theology of the pandemic   11

The dark power
    C.S. Lewis 13

Faith and fear
    Paul Kraus 14

Covid-19 lockdown
    Paul Kraus 16

The pandemic and theology
    Tomáš Halík 18

Silent questions
    Paul Kraus 27

Working for a purpose
    Gerard Manley Hopkins 28

Learning from Covid-19 that we are not alone...
    Teresa Anyabuike 29

Locating our invisible wounds
    Leah Libresco Sergeant 30

A prayer for our uncertain times
    William Barber 33

Pandemic
　　Lynn Ungar 34
Evolutionary hymn
　　C.S. Lewis 36
When the church doors close
　　Leslie Verner 38
Is this an apocalypse?
　　Catherine Keller and John J. Thatamanil 40
The Spirit of God prays in us
　　Henri Nouwen 45
Karl Rahner on what it means to love Jesus
　　Robert Imbelli 46
When words are not enough
　　Paul Kraus 51
God does not send us plagues to teach us things
　　Richard Leonard 53
Litany of solidarity and hope during a pandemic
　　Joseph P. Shadle 56
The theology of pandemics
　　Sam Ben Meir 58
Pope Francis shares his vision for Covid's aftermath
　　Gerard O'Connell 63
What am I to say?
　　Joseph Capizzi 67

Part 2　The love, power and prophetic voice of Christian mystics　　71

The love and power of Christian mystics: ancient and modern
　　Paul Kraus 72
Christ the physician
　　Augustine of Hippo 76

What can St Augustine teach us?
    Kathleen Bonnette 78

Our life, our hope, our healing
    Source unknown 82

Julian of Norwich: the plague and the pandemic
    Paul Kraus 83

Julian of Norwich speaks about our earth
    Veronica Mary Rolf 86

Stillness, silence...
    Paul Kraus 88

A prayer for those suffering from the coronavirus
    Catholic Health Association of America 90

Peace prayer of St Francis
    Fr Esther Bouquerel (1855-1923) 91

A Franciscan benediction
    Richard Rohr 92

Teresa of Avila and John of the Cross
    Paul Kraus 93

St John of the Cross
    Paul Kraus 98

Conversation of the heart
    Paul Kraus 102

Defying the Covid pandemic
    Dorothy Day and Hudson Taylor 104

Inner attitude: a barometer of our health
    Paul Kraus 105

Thomas Merton – new seeds of spiritual direction
and growth
    Paul Kraus 107

Peace and joy in the midst of uncertainty
    Book of Common Praise 110

Love alone overcomes fear
  Paul Kraus 112

Returning to the heart
  Laurence Freeman 116

A prayer for healing
  Mark Coleridge 118

A time for regeneration
  Peter Mommsen 119

A better way is possible
  Christopher Lamb 122

A holy moment
  Paul Kraus 126

The everlasting mercy
  John Masefield 128

About the author 129

Acknowledgments 131

A Christian world view

In 1937, the famous English poet T. S. Eliot differentiated the Christian outlook from the pagan by this point: the Christian looks not merely towards some external evil or 'other' but acknowledges the inherent evil within the result of our fallen nature in need of conversion. We are called to prayer and penance, and only then can we assert ourselves, publicly profess our faith and traditions and refuse to apologise for them. The creed does not begin by what we fear, nor what we oppose, but by what we believe: the truths we are willing to die for.

> I heard an angel singing
> When the day was springing
> Mercy, Pity and Peace
> Are the world's release.

William Blake The Two Songs

Foreword

We have entered a strange landscape in the world of COVID-19. We didn't see it coming and we don't know where it is taking us. We struggle to find our bearings as we seek a balance between the demands of public health, the requirements of compassion and the needs of the economy. The physical and social threats are real enough, but so too are the emotional, psychological and spiritual threats of the pandemic.

That's why it's good that Paul Kraus offers here a symphony of voices – his own among them – that can help us chart a course through this bewildering time. He draws upon voices of the past, voices of people who themselves knew times of affliction. But we also hear voices of our own time who know our own anxiety and distress, our questions and uncertainties. We hear voices from literature, theology and spirituality, voices from the heart of the Church and voices from the edge. They speak from different parts of the world, but always in recognisably human accents which speak to every heart.

In exploring the theology and spirituality of the pandemic this collection takes us beyond the standard discussion and usual coverage to the deeper point where the wound is identified and the healing is found. In the end, the focus is on Jesus Christ crucified and risen, who has borne all our wounds and in whom there is eternal healing.

Foreword

I thank Paul Kraus for producing this work which is the tip of an iceberg. What is found here is the fruit of personal prayer, wide reading and patient reflection, only some of which finds its way into the words. May this unique collection serve as a source of encouragement and insight for all who read it, so that on a journey that can at times be gloomy, a shaft of Easter light may break through to show us the way into the future.

✠ Mark Coleridge
Archbishop of Brisbane.

Introduction

We currently live in a world where the media is centred on the social dislocation and pain caused by the COVID-19 pandemic that allegedly began in China and spread to western nations in early 2020. Disruption, isolation, unemployment and, of course, widespread suffering and loss has been repeatedly in the headlines. All churches closed their doors, in response to government health directives. As with all other aspects of our lives, religious life has been forced to change its way of worship, which came to be online.

This book is a compilation of poems, brief essays and sayings from well-known Christian thinkers such as C.S. Lewis, saints, mystics and others who have left their mark on history. Most, if not all, the voices in the book include some kind of answer to our seemingly intractable current problems. The saints and mystics, whose writings are featured in the following pages include Francis of Assisi, Julian of Norwich, Teresa of Avila and the poet, John of the Cross. Other influential voices are recalled from recent Christian history, such as Thomas Merton, Henri Nouwen, Karl Rahner and Richard Rohr.

Healing in its fullness, shown in the stories of Jesus in the Gospel records, brings true wellness to serve our physical and spiritual reality. This is also the theme of this collection. The sub-title of this book, *Locating Our Invisible Wounds*, is significant. We are introduced to the basic theology of this pandemic, through the provocative and challenging essay by

Introduction

Professor Tomáš Halík, a theologian, academic and priest from the Czech Republic. He writes in a simple style about the world we currently inhabit and suggests answers to some long-standing problems, especially a challenge to the Church to reach out to spiritual 'seekers.'

The second part of the book, *The Love, Power and Prophetic Voice of Christian Mystics*, stresses that social isolation is not the only law to be heeded in regard to the spreading of this illness. The relationship of the individual to his/her brothers and sisters, to our neighbours, is also vital. The element of true charity, in conformity to our Lord, is also expressed in poetry, prayers and stories.

Jesus, our risen Lord and eternal Christ, is shown as the only one who can provide hope and healing to this broken world. Jesus repeatedly spoke to people in need throughout the gospels, especially in parables. He was, at times, pitiful and sad. He was always wise in the way he spoke not only to his followers, but to various people who crossed his path. Ultimately, his death was meaningful in the realm of human history. Atonement was forever re-defined and we can all be recipients to Jesus as Lord and as our eternal Christ.

In his brief ministry, Jesus was primarily a healer, not merely of physical illness, but of emotional problems as well. A number of gospel stories point to this fact. Where else can we find answers to the infinite problems we face, except in the ministry of Jesus, our Master, our Saviour in every realm, shown beautifully and bountifully in the Gospel stories. The poems, essays and words in this volume all point to Jesus, the healer of our lives, the healer of our world.

Will we ever 'go back to normal' in this fractured society and disparate world that the coronavirus pandemic has initiated? This is a key question about the how and the why of change in our society, with the devastation of our economy and the massive job redundancies. Suffering and dislocation are evident at every social and economic level right across the globe. The statistics of those suffering from COVID-19, here in Australia, but far more dramatically in the United Kingdom, Europe and in both the United States and nations like Brazil in South America are frightening.

This writing points to new directions for the people of God. The Church must take heed of this message of regeneration at this 'holding' time of the world coronavirus pandemic. The Church continues its work of love, mercy, healing and wholeness to broken people, whether or not they are affected by this virus throughout the world in which we live.

The encouraging, hopeful, straightforward and powerful positive words of Pope Francis in his *Urbi et Orbi* message over Easter 2020, when he addressed this universal problem of our 'plague', is recorded and commented on in these pages.

I sincerely hope that all who read the numerous messages in the book will be informed not only about the impact of the COVID pandemic conveyed but inspired by the love, power and wisdom of 'saints and sinners' saints, mystics, poets and prophets of other ages and our own. I also hope that the reader might find a few gems of inspiration within these pages. May God bless all those who read these words spoken mainly by people of another age, those who have been before us on this, our earthly pilgrimage.

Paul Kraus

Part 1

The theology of the pandemic

The dark power

What is the problem? A universe that contains much that is obviously bad and apparently meaningless, but containing creatures like ourselves who know that it is bad and meaningless. There are only two views that face all the facts. One is the Christian view that this is a good world that has gone wrong, but still retains the memory of what it ought to have been. The other is the view called Dualism. Dualism means the belief that there are two equal and independent powers at the back of everything, one of them good and the other bad, and that the universe is the battlefield in which they fight out an endless war...

One of the things that surprised me when I first read the New Testament seriously was that it talked so much about a Dark Power in the universe a mighty evil spirit who was held to be the Power behind death and disease, and sin. The difference is that Christianity thinks this dark Power was created by God, and was good when he was created, and went wrong. Christianity agrees with dualism that this universe is at war, But it does not think this is a war between independent powers. It thinks it is a civil war, a rebellion, and that we are living in a part of the universe occupied by the rebel.

C.S. Lewis

(From C.S. Lewis, *Mere Christianity*)

Faith and fear

> For men are homesick in their homes,
> And strangers under the sun,
> And they lay their heads in a foreign land
> Whenever the day is done.
>
> G.K. Chesterton

Good Friday ends solemnly with death itself, yet the life
and light of Easter forever dispels life's darkness.

Finality briefly drifts in this currency of mortal dissent
as a coronavirus pandemic spreads starkness

across us all, running rampant, an unwieldy knife tears
at bodies and souls in every land, still no healer found.

Humanity curves, creepy fingers crawl throughout these awful fears:
elderly, middle aged, yet those in youthful years.

This phantom speaks with silent animosity in endless gall, a virus
whose origins unknown confounds our computerised world.

Social distance, lockdowns, hygiene the aggregate of all:
these strategies in order to save us from catastrophe.

Universal pandemic shatters society, stratifies our world,
yet brings hope of goodness, wellness when happiness is redefined.

Faith and fear

Some may wonder what our future holds, economies decline,
unfolding burdens of a war-like kind, leaving souls alone,

faithless, shattered, all simply gone, without light or hope.
Frailty and fear, set against the beauty and glory of this Easter light.

Happy are those who cannot see, yet still believe...
people only know this certainty beyond our time-bound reality.

A living faith, where hearts and minds rejoice, give praise
in love we know Christ our Lord, who reigns forevermore.

Paul Kraus

This poem was written over Easter 2020, after the Covid-19 lockdown had been announced when there was a widespread feeling of consternation and fear in the community.

Covid-19 lockdown

Like a lost prodigal child whose thoughts
are cast away … foolhardy … negative
in all kinds of ways: rejecting desires,
plans pushed aside in favour of finer days
when social distancing is left behind,
Covid–19 merely an ongoing memory.

Then again routine is worshipped
as life is 'just the same again':
now fully digitalised and rearranged
in this computerised world.
Are values just the same or somehow
changed in this post-viral age?

Material priorities loom large as life,
indeed the government strives
to stop more economic strife
to all who followed the job keepers
slender life, now tries to survive
and become the heaven of self-sufficiency.

Not quite apocalyptic, to borrow
a theological term: this unveiling,
so they say, yet in a sense of sorrow
to expose our non-sustaining world
for our failing world we ask how
this pandemic is at all an apocalypse.

Covid-19 lockdown

Where will our future lie in this world,
quite as rife as when the Spanish Flu,
the Plague and other calamities were
hardly solved when here again not a clue
In this age of medical miracles, vague
we clearly hope to find a new vaccine.

God's mysteries still pertain in this unheard time,
his angels, saints and all beyond mysteriously
present and ask of this global suffering,
this line of physical, spiritual, material dissent.
What catastrophe or timelessness
will stay in this new world, our sanctuary?

Paul Kraus

The pandemic and theology

Christianity at a time of sickness

Our world is sick. I'm not just referring to the coronavirus pandemic, but to the state of our civilisation, as revealed in this global phenomenon. In biblical terms: a sign of the times.

At the beginning of this unusual period of Lent, many of us thought that this epidemic would cause a sort of short-term blackout, a breakdown in the usual operation of society, one that we would ride out somehow, and then soon things would all return to the way they were. They won't. And it wouldn't turn out well if we tried. After this global experience, the world won't be the same as it was before, and it probably oughtn't to be.

It is natural at times of major calamities that we first concern ourselves with the material necessities for survival; but 'one does not live by bread alone'. The time has come to examine the deeper implications of this blow to the security of our world. The unavoidable process of globalisation would seem to have peaked: the global vulnerability of a global world is now plain to see.

The church as a field hospital

What kind of challenge does this situation represent for Christianity and the church – one of the first 'global players' – and for theology?

The church should be a 'field hospital' as proposed by Pope Francis. The pope means by this metaphor that the church should not remain in splendid isolation from the world but should break free of its boundaries and give help where people are physically, mentally, socially and spiritually afflicted. Yes, this is how the church can do penance for the wounds inflicted by its representatives recently on the most defenceless. But let us try to think more deeply about this metaphor – and put it into practice.

If the church is to be a 'hospital', it must, of course, offer the health, social and charitable care it has offered since the dawn of its history. But as a good hospital, the church must also fulfil other tasks. It has a diagnostic role to play (identifying the 'signs of the times'), a preventive role (creating an 'immune system' in a society in which the malignant viruses of fear, hatred, populism and nationalism are rife) and a convalescent role (overcoming the traumas of the past by forgiveness).

Empty churches as a sign of change

Before Easter last year, Notre Dame cathedral in Paris burned down. This year in Lent there are no services in hundreds of thousands of churches on several continents, nor in synagogues and mosques. As a priest and a theologian, I reflect on those empty or closed churches as a sign and a challenge from God.

Understanding the language of God in the events of our world requires the art of spiritual discernment, which in turn calls for contemplative detachment from our heightened emotions and our prejudices, as well as from the projections of our fears and desires. At moments of disaster, the 'sleeping agents of a wicked, vengeful God' spread fear, and make religious capital out of it for themselves. Their vision of God has been grist to the mill of atheism for centuries.

At a time of disasters, I don't see God as an ill-tempered director, sitting comfortably backstage as the events of our world play out, but instead I look on him as a source of strength, operating in those who show solidarity and self-sacrificing love in such situations – yes, including those who have no 'religious motivation' for their action. God is humble and discreet love.

But I can't help wondering whether the time of empty and closed churches is not some kind of cautionary vision of what might happen in the fairly near future: this is what it could look like in a few years' time in a large part of our world. Haven't we already had plenty of warning from the developments in many countries, where more and more churches, monasteries and priestly seminaries have been emptying and closing? Why have we been ascribing this development for so long to outside influences (the 'secularist tsunami'), instead of realising that another chapter in the history of Christianity is coming to a close, and it is time to prepare for a new one.

Maybe this time of empty church buildings symbolically exposes the churches' hidden emptiness and their possible future unless they make a serious attempt to show the world a completely different face of Christianity. We have thought too much about converting 'the world' ('the rest'), and less about converting ourselves – not simply 'improvement', but a radical change from a static 'being Christians' to a dynamic 'becoming Christians'.

When the medieval church made excessive use of the interdict as a penalty, and those 'general strikes' by the entire ecclesiastical machinery meant that church services were not held and sacraments were not administered, people started increasingly to seek a personal relationship with God, a 'naked faith'. Lay fraternities and mysticism proliferated. That upsurge of mysticism definitely helped pave the way for the Reformation – not only Luther's and Calvin's but also the Catholic reformation connected with the Jesuits and Spanish mysticism. Maybe discovery of contemplation could help complement the 'synodal path' to a new reforming council.

A call for reform

Maybe we should accept the present abstinence from religious services and the operation of the church as *kairos*, an opportunity to stop and engage in thorough reflection before God and with God. I am convinced the time has come to reflect on how to continue the path of reform, which Pope Francis says is necessary: not attempts to return to a world that no longer exists, or reliance just on external structural reforms, but instead a shift towards the heart of the Gospel, 'a journey into the depths'.

I can't see that a quick fix in the form of artificial substitutes, such as the broadcasting of Masses, will be a good solution at this time when public worship is banned. A shift to 'virtual piety', 'remote communion', and kneeling in front of a TV screen is truly something odd. Maybe we should instead test the truth of Jesus's words: where two or three gather in my name, I am there with them.

Did we really think that we could solve the lack of priests in Europe by importing 'spare parts' for the church's machinery from seemingly bottomless storehouses in Poland, Asia and Africa? Of course, we must take seriously the proposals of the Amazonian synod, but we need at the same time to provide greater scope for the ministry of laypeople in the church; let us not forget that in many territories the church survived without clergy for entire centuries.

Maybe this 'state of emergency' is an indicator of the new face of the church, for which there is a historical precedent. I am convinced that our Christian communities, parishes, congregations, church movements and monastic communities should seek to draw closer to the ideal that gave rise to the European universities: a community of pupils and teachers, a school of wisdom, in which truth is sought through free disputation and also profound contemplation. Such islands of spirituality and dialogue could be the source of a healing force for a sick world. The day before the papal election, Cardinal Bergoglio quoted a passage from Revelation in which Jesus stands before the door and knocks. He added: Today Christ is knocking from inside the church and wants to get out. Maybe that is what he just did.

Where is the Galilee to-day?

For years I have pondered on the well-known text of Friedrich Nietzsche's about the 'mad man' (the fool who alone is permitted to speak the truth) proclaiming 'the death of God'. That chapter ends with the madman coming to church to sing 'Requiem aeternam Deo' and asking: 'What after all are these churches now if they are not the tombs and sepulchres of God?' I must admit that for a long time, various forms of the church seemed to me like cold and opulent sepulchres of a dead god.

It looks as if many of our churches will be empty at Easter this year. We will read the gospel passages about the empty tomb somewhere else. If the emptiness of the churches is reminiscent of the empty tomb, let us not ignore the voice from above: 'He is not here. He has risen. He has gone ahead of you to Galilee'.

A question to stimulate meditation for this strange Easter: Where is the Galilee of today, where we can encounter the living Christ?

Sociological research indicates that in the world, the number of 'dwellers' (both those who fully identify with the traditional form of religion, and those who assert a dogmatic atheism) is falling, while there is an increase in the number of 'seekers'. In addition, of course, there is a rise in the number of 'apatheists' – people who couldn't care less about religious issues or the traditional response to them.

The main dividing line is no longer between those who consider themselves believers and those who consider themselves non-believers. There are 'seekers' among believers (those for whom faith is not a 'legacy' but a 'way'), and among 'non-believers', who reject the religious notions put forward to them by those around them, but nevertheless have a yearning for something to satisfy their thirst for meaning.

I am convinced that the 'Galilee of today', where we must seek God, who has survived death, is the world of the seekers.

Seeking Christ among seekers

Liberation Theology taught us to seek Christ among people on the fringes of society. But it is also necessary to seek him among people marginalised within the church, among those 'who don't follow us'. If we want to connect with them as Jesus' disciples, there are many things we must first abandon.

We must abandon many of our former notions about Christ. The Resurrected One is radically transformed by the experience of death. As we read in the Gospels, even his nearest and dearest did not recognise him. We don't have to accept at all the news that surrounds us. We can persist in wanting to touch his wounds. Besides, where else will we be sure to encounter them than in the wounds of the world and the wounds of the church, in the wounds of the body that he took on himself?

We must abandon our proselytising aims. We are not entering the world of the seekers to 'convert' them as quickly as possible and squeeze them into the existing institutional and mental confines of our churches. Jesus also didn't try to squeeze those 'lost sheep of the house of Israel' back into the structures of the Judaism of his day. He knew that new wine must be poured into new wineskins.

We want to take new and old things from the treasure house of tradition that we have been entrusted with, and make them part of a dialogue with seekers, a dialogue in which we can and should learn from each other. We must learn to broaden radically the boundaries of our understanding of the church. It is no longer enough for us to magnanimously open a 'court of the Gentiles'. The Lord has already knocked 'from within' and come out – and it is our job to seek him and follow him. Christ has passed through the door that we had locked out of fear of others. He has passed through the wall that we surrounded ourselves with. He has opened up a space whose breadth and depth has made us dizzy.

On the very threshold of its history, the early church of Jews and pagans experienced the destruction of the temple in which Jesus prayed and taught his disciples. The Jews of those days found a courageous and creative solution: they replaced the altar of the demolished temple with the Jewish family table, and the practice of sacrifice with the practice of private and communal prayer. They replaced burnt offerings and blood sacrifices with 'lip sacrifice': reflection, praise, and study of

Scripture. Around the same time, early Christianity, banished from the synagogue, sought a new identity of its own. On the ruins of traditions, Jews and Christians learnt anew to read the Law and the prophets and interpret them afresh. Aren't we in a similar situation in our days?

God in all things

When Rome fell on the threshold of the fifth century, there was an instant explanation from many quarters: the pagans saw it as punishment of the gods for the adoption of Christianity, while the Christians saw it as God's punishment on Rome, for continuing to be the whore of Babylon. St Augustine rejected both those interpretations: at that watershed moment, he developed his theology of the age-old battle between two opposing 'cities': not of Christians and pagans, but of two 'loves' dwelling in the human heart: the love of self, closed to transcendence (*amor sui usque ad contemptum Dei*) and love that gives of itself and thereby finds God (*amor Dei usque ad contemptum sui*). Doesn't this time of civilisational change call for a new theology of contemporary history and a new understanding of the church?

'We know where the church is, but we don't know where she isn't,' the orthodox theologian Evdokimov taught. Maybe what the last Council said about catholicity and ecumenism needs to acquire a deeper content. It is time for a broader and deeper ecumenism, for a bolder 'search for God in all things'.

We can, of course, accept this Lent of empty and silent churches as simply a brief temporary measure soon to be forgotten. But we can also embrace it as *kairos* – an opportune moment 'to put into deeper water' and seek a new identity for Christianity in a world which is being radically transformed before our eyes. The current pandemic is certainly not the only global threat facing our world now and in the future.

Let us embrace the approaching Eastertide as a challenge to seek Christ anew. Let us not seek the Living among the dead. Let us seek him boldly and tenaciously, and let us not be taken aback if he appears to us as a foreigner. We will recognise him by his wounds, by his voice when he speaks to us intimately, by the Spirit that brings peace and banishes fear.

Tomáš Halík

Tomáš Halík(b. 1948) is a professor of sociology at Charles University, Prague, President of the Czech Christian Academy, and university chaplain. During the Communist regime, he was active in the 'underground church'. He is a Templeton Prize laureate and holds an honorary doctorate from Oxford University.

(Personal permission gained to reproduce this essay from Professor Tomáš Halík.)

Silent questions

Pandemic virus lies everywhere, the reason for empty churches
here and there: now online, temporarily they seem silhouettes of peace.
Where is hope in such unknown times: apocalypse, privacy or prophecy?

Questions plead from this act of freedom: God is power, not weakness,
in whom we contemplate, adore, love as searching ceases.
What meaning lies within this worldwide mystery, a bleakness found.

Globally moralistic minds survive and ask what new chapter
speaks from this religious history, when so few celebrate
the churches year: an unknown power, the glory of a living God.

What purpose lies within these empty walls when services still prevail?
Kairos, knowledge and insight on earth as in heaven this pandemic
sent ... not a requiem, or for anyone else to assail.

He is not here, a voice in heaven proclaims: no mysterious
message, yet a victory that Easter forever will proclaim.
History asks the meaning of this world's new sounds.

No longer pigeonholed by media's laws, agendas arrive at every stage
in each nation's realm, yet in all the world precious gifts will abound:
how will the prosperity gospel sell or bring eternal change?

Will a reformation come within the page of this computer age?
History no longer rules with vastly different needs.
Now a spiritual thirst remains in this material world.

Sanctity and holiness, hardly seen, felt, known in this material world:
wonder, spirituality belong only to a tiny few, yet this pandemic asks
questions that will ring and last, everlasting, unchanging eternal truths.

Paul Kraus

Working for a purpose

To lift up hands in prayer gives God glory, but a man with a dung fork in his hand, a woman with a shop pail, give him glory too. He is so great that all things give him glory if you mean they should. It is not only prayer that gives glory but work. Smiting an anvil, sawing a beam, whitewashing a wall, driving horses, sweeping, scouring everything gives God some glory if being in his grace you do it as your duty.

Gerard Manley Hopkins (1844-1889), Jesuit poet

Learning from Covid-19 that we are not alone...

What started innocently enough, then swept a country and gradually crept into other countries, has become a universal problem that knows no border.

Covid-19 has made me realise more and more that we're all God's children in a world that is divided by arbitrary lines on a 'map'. This virus does not know border, race, sex or any other name which we use to divide ourselves into categories. Covid-19 has kept me thinking of how interconnected we are.

The virus brings tears to my eyes. I hold in my heart families that have lost dear ones - not able to say goodbye or mourn properly countries struggling to care for their sick, families crowded in a room, caregivers being infected, people losing their jobs and becoming unable to provide for their families. People are afraid to touch or embrace one another.

I ask, 'When will this end?' I guess I don't have the answer.

The only thing I do know is to keep hope alive and trust in Divine Providence.

Teresa Anyabuike, Sister of Notre Dame de Namur,

Ilorin, Kwara State, Nigeria.

(Taken from Global Sisters Report, 25 May 2020, National Catholic Reporter.)

(Permission gained from the editor of The Global Sisters Report.)

Locating our invisible wounds

Confronting our blindness before and after the virus.

There's something cheering about walking around my neighbourhood and seeing people swerve into the street or climb into flowerbeds to allot each other our six feet of safety. Even though I can only see eyes crinkle above masks in lieu of smiles, every action communicates, 'I'm taking care of you. We're in this together'.

The crisis has made us all look at each other more closely. In a time of lockdown, it's the people nearest us, whom we may not have known or chosen deliberately, whom we have to rely on. The pandemic is pushing us past the limits of whom we previously trusted or entrusted ourselves to, and we have the opportunity to learn to extend ourselves in love, even when we no longer are forced to.

At present, no-one feels like a stranger, since the biggest thing in all our lives right now is shared, and known to be shared. Any pair of people passing may have very different levels of risk, and one may be more worried for his health while another is more concerned about her laid-off employees. But both know that the other one is swept up in the same storm. And that camaraderie isn't specific to the coronavirus crisis. Rebecca Solnit, in her book on solidarity in disasters, *A Paradise Built in Hell*, contrasted the feeling of unity in shared suffering with the isolation of individual catastrophe. She highlights the work of sociologist Charles Fritz, who compared widespread disaster with the way people 'suffer and die daily, though in ordinary times, they do so privately, separately'.

The coronavirus crisis hits hardest the already vulnerable. It makes them suffer, but it also restores them to visibility. The grandmother in a nursing home running with insufficient staff; the children who rely on free school lunch to be able to eat; the warehouse worker, who, despite taking extra shifts, is still one of the 40 per cent of Americans who couldn't raise the cash to cover a $400 expense on short notice. Those vulnerabilities will persist long after a vaccine.

Pope Francis reminded the world in his out-of-season *Urbi et Orbi* blessing, that the unusual suffering caused by the novel coronavirus should also draw our attention to the suffering we ignore because it is not novel. He said, 'We did not stop at God's reproach to us, we were not shaken awake by wars or injustice across the world, nor did we listen to the cry of the poor or of our ailing planet. We carried on regardless, thinking we would stay healthy in a world that was sick'.

His prayers aren't focused on simply returning to normal, since in the 'normal' world, many people live through daily, lonely cataclysms. We are called to retain our present sense of solidarity, and, if we love our neighbour as ourselves, to enter into their suffering and need, even when, especially when, it becomes a choice again.

The Pope gave his blessing with nearly a life-sized crucifix behind him. The wounded Christ looked out with him into the empty St Peter's Square. The crucifixion makes visible the full cost of sin. Every spiteful word, every charity withheld from the needy, every lustful look reducing someone else to a thing, wounded its immediate target invisibly, but that harm is shown in Christ's flesh on the cross.

At the present time, we also struggle to see the face of God in our neighbour not because we are tempted to hate our neighbour, but because we have already glimpsed our neighbour's face. We have sought each other out in the present moment of extremis.

In the grip of the virus, our collective suffering is unchosen, forced on us. In the days and months to come, we have a responsibility to retain the present sense of compassion, which means 'to suffer with'. As stores eventually reopen, and parks fill again, we have to remember and search for the people whose need was particularly acute in the pandemic, but for whom 'normal' is still a slow-moving disaster.

Leah Libresco Sargeant, *Comment Journal*, 4 June 2020
(*Used by permission of the editor Comment Journal*)

A prayer for our uncertain times

May we who are merely inconvenienced remember those whose lives are at stake.

May we who have no risk factors remember those most vulnerable.

May we who have the luxury of working from home remember those who must choose between preserving their health and making their rent.

May we who have the flexibility to care for our children when their schools close remember those who have no options.

May we who have to cancel our trips remember those who have no safe place to go.

May we who are losing our margin money in the tumult of the economic market remember those who have no margin at all.

May we who settle in for a quarantine at home remember those who have no home.

As fear grips our country, let us choose love.

And during this time when we may not be able to physically wrap our arms around each other, let us yet find ways to be the loving embrace of God to our neighbours. Amen.

William Barber,
Prayers During the Coronavirus Pandemic
www.jesuitsources.org, 11 March 2020

Pandemic

What if you thought of it
as the Jews consider the Sabbath
the most sacred of times?
Cease from travel.
Cease from buying and selling.
Give up, just for now,
on trying to make the world
different than it is.
Sing. Pray. Touch only those
to whom you commit your life.
Centre down.

And when your body has become still,
reach out with your heart.
Know that we are connected
in ways that are terrifying and beautiful.
(You could hardly deny it now.)
Know that our lives
are in one another's hands.
(Surely, that has become clear.)
Do not reach out your hands.
Reach out your heart.
Reach out your words.
Reach out all the tendrils
of compassion that move, invisibly,
where we cannot touch.

Promise this world your love
for better or for worse,
in sickness and in health,
so long as we all shall live.

> Lynn Ungar, poet and writer.
>
> California. March 2020
>
> (*Used with the permission of the poet*)

Evolutionary hymn

Up the future's endless stair;
Chop us, change us, prod us, weed us.
For stagnation is despair:
Groping, guessing, yet progressing,
Lead us nobody knows where.

Wrong or justice, joy or sorrow,
In the present what are they
While there's always jam to-morrow,
While we tread the onward way?
Never knowing where we're going,
We can never go astray.

To whatever variation
Our posterity may turn
Hairy, squashy, or crustacean,
Bulbous-eyed or square of stern,
Tusked or toothless, mild or ruthless,
Towards that unknown god we yearn.

Ask not if it's god or devil,
Brethren, lest your words imply
Static norms of good and evil
(As in Plato) throned on high;
Such scholastic,
Abstract yardsticks we deny.

Far too long have sages vainly
Glossed great Nature's simple text:

Evolutionary hymn

He who runs can hear it plainly,
'Goodness equals what comes next'.
By evolving, Life is solving
All the questions we perplexed.
Oh then! Value means survival
Value. If our progeny
Spreads and spawns and licks each rival,
That will prove its deity
Far from pleasant, by our present,
Standards, though it may be well.

C.S. Lewis.
(*Used with permission*)

When the church doors close

The severe mercies of social isolation

I wasn't permitted to attend church for three years while I lived in northwest China. Our city did not have a government-sanctioned church and my organisation didn't allow us to attend non-government (underground) churches. Instead, I met with one other American and we took turns planning the 'services'. We would stream sermons, read scripture, sing hymns, and listen to worship songs online. Our version of church looked much like many of the services I saw streamed last Sunday, but a bit more homegrown. Despite longing for corporate worship at the time, I now look back with nostalgia at the simplicity of those days. The sacred ritual of church was distilled down to its bare essentials.

How can those who are able to stay at home with ease find ways to serve the vulnerable from a social distance? We no longer have the luxury of proximity. Since this illness is spread through contact, the best way to love others is to keep our distance. That said, we can still check in via text message, video calls or email. We can donate to local charities and food banks. If we're buying groceries, we can offer to do this for our elderly or immunocompromised friends and family. We can donate hospital supplies or order take-away for hospital staff. Need is demanding increased ingenuity and creativity as we love from a distance.

In *Acedia and Me*, Kathleen Norris writes: 'For grace to be grace, it must give us things we didn't know we needed and take us to places where we didn't want to go..' None of us would have chosen this pandemic. But after the carving away, stripping down, isolating and daily reminders of our mortality, how much more will we revel in the physical comfort of a hug frim a friend? One writer has called Lent a 'season of darkness', yet Easter is called 'a season of hope'. Dietrich Bonhoeffer writes in *Life Together* that 'after a time of quiet we meet others in a different and fresh way'. Imagine the feasts we'll celebrate when we creep out from our tombs and revel in the gift of togetherness again.

When I returned to the United States after years of not experiencing corporate worship in China, I worshipped with a crowd again in my Chicago church. I stretched up my ams as we sang, tears pouring down my face. My social isolation had increased my gratitude for the communal worship I had once taken for granted. Perhaps the church will discover fresh ways to exhibit love to a frightened world and unearth some startling mercies during this horrific and holy season of uncertainty.

Leslie Verner
Plough Quarterly Magazine, 3 April 2020.
(*Used by permission*)

Is this an apocalypse?

The Covid-19 pandemic has many Christian communities wondering if the Apocalypse has finally arrived. We very much hope so.

No, we are not Christian fundamentalists praying to precipitate calamitous world-ending conflict and mass death in order to hasten Jesus's return a perverse vision by any standard (and not our idea of 'end times fun!'). Despite its endless misreading for purposes of vengeful violence or end time fatalism, the metaphor of the apocalypse is back to stay. Even without the pandemic, climate change has reheated its relevance.

Therefore, we suspect that a moment's attention to the actual ancient meaning of apocalypse may make for more responsible uses, secular or spiritual as a warning, a wake-up call at the edge of time. Of *our* time.

Contemporaries keep using the term 'apocalypse', but literalist biblical interpretation notwithstanding, the term doesn't mean what many think it means. Deriving from the Greek *apokalypsis*, the word means 'unveiling' or 'revelation'. Hence, the title given to the final book of the Christian Bible, 'The Apocalypse of John', is accurately translated 'Revelation' not 'Cataclysm'. Not 'The End'. Unfortunately, this root meaning has been forgotten in popular circles.

When the term is understood as 'unveiling,' we can then ask the right questions: What does this pandemic unveil? What have we refused to see about ourselves and the precarious world we've built, a world that now stands exposed and tottering in the harsh light of this unasked-for revelation? If we permit this crisis to expose the fissures of our failing world, this pandemic will have served as properly *apocalyptic*. If, instead, despite its devastating toll, we return to an obsolete and unsustainable world, nothing meaningful will have been revealed.

As for the Book of Revelation, it too does not contain what popular depictions suggest. To begin with, credible biblical scholarship indicates that the author, John of Patmos, was not writing about the end of *our* world, but the end of *his*.

Writing as a member of a marginalised and persecuted religious community of Jesus followers at the end of the first century of the Common Era, John and his community witnessed the destruction of the city of Jerusalem, the fall of its hallowed temple, and the dispersion of its peoples, all instigated by Rome's imperial brutality. Under such circumstances, writing openly and critically about Roman imperialism would have proved deadly for the author and his community. That is why John marshals a baroque and elusive symbolic repertoire for his audience an audience who could easily decipher its dreamlike code.

If John was writing about *his* epoch, how are the particular symbols of the apocalypse relevant today, two millennia later?

John was not 'predicting' this moment. Prophecy is not prediction of this or any closed future. Rather, prophecy is the poetic unveiling of underlying patterns patterns of civilisation so deep that they may replicate themselves indefinitely, until they bring on some climactic self-destruction. In John's Revelation, destruction takes planetary form. So, for instance, upon the opening of the 'seventh seal', after 'half an hour of silence' is held in heaven: 'a third of the earth was burned up, and a third of the trees were burned up'. How can one not flash to the Amazon, then Australia, over the past few months?

Then, 'a third of the living creatures in the sea died'. Are we there yet? What with current warming, acidification, plastic pollution, dying coral reefs, threatened phytoplankton that produce half the world's oxygen ask an oceanographer.

No, John was not foreseeing climate change. He was dream-reading a tendency of human systems to bring down the nonhuman ones that support us. On the civilisational system, his code gets very pointed: the '666' tattooed on the head of the Beast signals in the ancient Hebrew gematria code 'NeroCaesar,' encrypting the legacy of imperial violence.

On the back of this political power rides the 'Whore of Babylon'. What system does she pornographically symbolise? All too literally clear: John lists twenty-nine luxury products of Roman world trade from gold, wine, olive oil to slaves. If the beast signifies imperialist politics, Babylon signifies not the consuming debauchery of neoliberal capitalism, but of its ancestor, the imperial global economy. He suddenly turns on her, devours her, bringing down the whole system. The 'merchants weep' at global economic collapse.

No, John wasn't *predicting* our present economic crisis; he was just dream-reading a deep contradiction at the heart of human civilisation.

But at this moment, the apocalypse, flashing through the headlines, is about a systemic threat moving at much faster speed. At a gallop, you might say. In John's narrative it is the fourth horseman of horror, the one riding the pale green horse, who brings 'pestilence'. John was not predicting Covid-19. He was dream-reading world systems failure along with the plague, a familiar ancient catastrophe. That horse bears death by famine and wild animals. Its green pallor seems to embody the menace of the inhuman viral, agricultural, animal.

So what might coronavirus 'reveal' to us? Is it at once our inescapable interdependence with an earth-full of humans and nonhumans? Does that entanglement turn deadly when we repress it? When we think we can control, commodify and consume the matter of the world, does it bite back at our own mattering bodies?

In the vision, things don't get better before they get worse. The collapse of the civilisation built on systemic oppression and greed takes innumerable innocents 'including slaves' – down with it. Another figure of the nonhuman flies by: the eagle calling 'in a loud voice, woe, woe, woe to the inhabitants of the earth' (Revelation 8:13). All of them. It is a cry of profound grief for all earthlings. Is it not audible now across every 'social distance'?

Ancient warnings about ecological, economic and political horrors will continue to haunt our present tense. But as we tense up against what is yet to come, there is a last prophetic glint from the text.

Cataclysm catalyses radical change: it is figured as the city contrary to Rome/Babylon, a city gendered female, 'the New Jerusalem'. In this city, contrary to the world of The Wall, the gates are open 24/7. The image is built of the ancient Hebrew hope, rigorously historical and material, of 'the new heaven and earth'. In the biblical languages, 'heaven' means not something supernatural but earth's atmosphere as it extends into the mysterious darkness.

Perhaps, if we are able to awaken to what is unveiled in this apocalyptic moment, we will make our way forward into a new world rather than shore up the old one. John dream-read such a shift as sparklingly organic and diverse: the multiplicity of peoples, of nations, are renewed through the flow of clean water 'free for all to drink' and to wash their hands frequently!

And 'the leaves of the trees are for the healing of the nations' (Revelation 22:2). If you've read Richard Powers' novel *The Overstory*, the new arboreal botany, or the movement to plant billions of trees, the metaphor matters. Trees extract excess CO_2 from the atmosphere and grant us breathing space and breathing time. Not that trees will 'fix' climate change for us, or water heal pandemics.

Neither will the biblical God conduct a rescue operation; for such intervention, we shouldn't hold our collective breath. Instead, some will seek to breathe in the Divine Spirit who may inspire us to find a way forward into a new world.

But what are the chances for a habitable and hospitably shared future? Close to none, if responsibility for the damage remains concealed. Which is why, even in the midst of flood, fire, or pandemic a way, a wisdom, can get revealed. Apocalypse after all? May it be so!

Catherine Keller,
George T. Cobb Professor of Constructive Theology
Drew University, Madison, New Jersey
John J. Thatamanil,
Associate Professor of Theology and World Religions
Union Theological Seminary, New York.

From *The Opinion*, 20 April 2020
(*Used with Permission from the A.B.C.*)

The Spirit of God prays in us

Silence means rest, rest of body and mind in which we become available for him whose heart is greater than ours. That is very threatening; it is like giving up control over our actions and thoughts, allowing something creative to happen not by us but to us. Is it so amazing that we are so often tired and exhausted, trying to be masters of ourselves, wanting to grasp the ultimate meaning of our existence, struggling with our identity? Silence is that moment in which we not only stop the discussion with others but also the inner discussions with ourselves, in which we can breathe in freely and accept our identity as a gift. 'Not I live, but he lives in me'.

It is in this silence that the Spirit of God can pray in us and continue his creative work in us. Without silence, the Spirit will die in us and the creative energy of our life will float away and leave.

Henri Nouwen

(*Reprinted by permission of The Henri Nouwen Society, May 2020*)

Karl Rahner on what it means to love Jesus

Karl Rahner was a German Jesuit priest and theologian whose ideas and work was influenced by Thomas Aquinas. The following essay outlines the comprehensiveness of our faith, not just from a sacramental viewpoint but in a broader sense in how it affects our lifestyle. The emphasis in this passage is on the relationship we can experience with Jesus in every aspect of our life. In the midst of a radical lifestyle change that the COVID-19 pandemic has forced universally upon us, we can locate our 'inner wounds' and live in total freedom as we walk on our pilgrim path.

Karl Rahner, S.J. was indisputably one of 20th century Catholicism's pre-eminent and most influential theologians. His long theological ministry spanned some fifty years, from the early 1930s until his death in 1984.

One of his writings that has always fascinated me is an essay entitled *'Christian Living Formerly and Today'*. The essay appeared just as the Second Vatican Council was ending at the end of 1965. He writes about the prophetic and often-quoted sentence: *'The devout Christian of the future will either be a 'mystic' someone who has 'experienced something' or will cease to be anything at all'*.

The essay strikes me as prophetic because in the ensuing fifty-five years since it first appeared, there has been a catastrophic decline in the Western world in the number of active and committed Catholics. To designate oneself as 'none' (at least from the religious point of view) can indeed sound like 'ceasing to be anything at all'.

The reasons for the decline in church numbers are many. They are both ecclesial and cultural. Guided by Rahner, one might ask: *Does it also indicate a deficit of 'experience?'* Put even more provocatively: *Is it the failure to actually become a 'mystic'* one who has experienced the faith at a certain depth and intensity?

Yet the Rahner essay also contains some perplexities. For example, it was always puzzling to me why Rahner said *'experience something,'* rather than *'experience Someone.'* For at the centre of Christian faith and life, formerly and today, is Jesus Christ. As the Letter to the Hebrews confesses: *'Jesus Christ, the same yesterday, today and for the ages'* a profession of faith notably echoed by the Second Vatican Council's *Gaudium et Spes*. At the very heart of St Paul's apostolic vocation lies his faith experience of the Lord Jesus, *'who loved me and gave himself for me'* (Galatians 2:20). And, in the Letter to the Ephesians, he prays earnestly that all the saints may come *'to know the love of Christ which surpasses knowledge'* and thus *'be filled with all the fullness of God'* (Ephesians 3:19).

Thus I was delighted when another essay by Rahner appeared some years later. In 1982, only two years before his death, he wrote an article entitled *'What Does It Mean to Love Jesus?'* Though dense, in the usual 'Rahnerian' manner, it focused explicitly upon the Christian's relation to his or her living saviour. Rahner insists: *'One can love Jesus, love him in himself, in true, genuine, immediate love'*. And he includes these remarkable words (spoken, he tells us, to the surprise of a rather *'rationalistic'* colleague): 'You're actually only really dealing with Jesus when you throw your arms around him and realise right down to the bottom of your being that this is something you can still do today'.

So the Christian of the future will be one who has experienced a life-changing encounter with the living Jesus Christ. As Pope Benedict XVI wrote in his first encyclical, *Deus Caritas Est*, 'Being Christian is not the result of an ethical choice or a lofty idea, but the encounter with an event, a person, who gives life a new horizon and a decisive direction'.

And this encounter gives rise to a relationship with Jesus that certainly admits of endless growth and deepening but is even now marked by intimate knowledge and love 'abiding' in him, as Jesus himself exhorts the disciples during the Farewell Discourse in John's Gospel. Indeed, as this relationship, this abiding matures, it more and more assumes the form of wholehearted attention to and affective embrace of the one whom one loves. Indeed, 'a throwing one's arms' about the Lord of one's life, as Rahner rather boldly declares to the evident dismay of his scholarly colleague.

Rahner certainly does not envision a 'physical' embrace. Nonetheless, the embrace of Jesus is uniquely 'tangible,' enlisting the full range of what the mystical tradition terms the 'spiritual senses.' One recalls Augustine's exultation in the magnificent Book Ten of his *Confessions*. Here Augustine struggles to give voice to the experience of his love for God and admits it far transcends physical sweetness or fragrance, brightness or beauty. And yet, he affirms: 'in a sense I do love light and melody and fragrance and food and embrace when I love my God... when that light shines upon my soul which no place can contain, that voice sounds which no time can take from me, when I breathe that fragrance which no wind scatters, I eat the food which is not lessened by eating, and I lie in that embrace which satiety never comes to sunder'.

Note how Augustine draws upon physical sensory experience – sight, hearing, tasting, touching – to point toward the experience of senses transformed so as to perceive the hidden but real presence of God in Christ. Thus Augustine confirms (or better 'inspires') Rahner's conviction that in the today of faith one can embrace the very Lord of life. For Augustine confesses that he could only find the way to the true God when he 'embraced the Mediator between God and man, the man Christ Jesus, who is above all things, God blessed forever,' yet who humbled himself to embody and become the believer's spiritual food and drink.

So we come to a final point worth noting. Two of Rahner's very first theological essays, dating from the early 1930s, studied the notion of the *'spiritual senses'* in the writings of the early church father Origen and in the medieval Augustinian tradition. It would seem, then, that Rahner returned toward the end of his life to those early explorations on the spiritual senses and the Christian mystical tradition. In doing so he returned to the wisdom of the concluding line of T. S. Eliot's *East Coker*: 'In my end is my beginning'.

Throughout his theological journey, Rahner sought to broaden our appreciation of the mystical, not as *'extracurricular'* to the Christian way, reserved for the privileged few, but as intrinsic to Christian living, yesterday and today. He challenges us to extend our imagination beyond the examples of those classical mystics who exhibit extraordinary spiritual gifts. He sought to *'democratise'* mystical experience, viewing it as the full flowering of the Christian life: a life of relations transformed in Christ, heralding the new creation. Though employing different dictions, I am sure Rahner would celebrate the insights of his fellow Jesuit, Gerard Manley Hopkins, S.J.

Purified senses enable us to perceive that *'Christ plays in ten thousand places, lovely in limbs, and lovely in eyes not his'*.

In and through all the intricacies of his signature *'transcendental method,'* Rahner's pole star remained the love of Jesus, who alone fulfils our human desire for unconditional love and communion. Communion not only with the Lord but also with all the members of his body. For loving Jesus is always inseparable from loving those who Jesus loves.

Robert Imbelli

From America, The Jesuit Review, 11 October 2020.
(Reproduced by permission of Fr Robert Imbelli.)

When words are not enough

In silence, God ceases to be an object and becomes an experience.

Thomas Merton

Opposite my window stands
a poinciana tree, a wise gentle
giant with its maternal stance.
Perfectly formed, congruent branches
where birds nest and sing their songs.
Calm, forever clear, forever strong.

I look at her frame in total tranquility,
in quietness and pure mindfulness.
Almost an icon, she sets my mind
aflame with love and peacefulness.
I see a lithesome, beautiful creation,
a stunning symbol, this completeness,
wholeness, wellness.
Musical, baroque, glorious harmony:
a life-giving spirit, a holiness
calmly washes over me.

I sometimes wonder if this grand tree
has intangible thoughts, or if she can see
the magnificence of her world.
Her silence brings strength and helps

me focus on the now.
She dispels distraction of ordinary words
and deeds, from unwarranted silly thoughts.
A simple time for keeping silent,
awareness wanders carelessly,
until stillness and quietness returns.

This tree, impartial guide, she never worries,
never tires, always calm, from a divine
architect she came. Unerring witness
perceiving untold truths of wisdom.
She is a silent spectator of our world,
giving meaning in this great loveliness.
Her simplicity embraces an abiding power.

This grandness, stillness, ethereal beauty,
spirituality, silence, whispers,
then softly speaks in times of healing,
hope and love. I humbly meditate,
contemplate this wonder ...
Calmness forever clear, forever strong ...
All is well... all is well... all is well.

Paul Kraus

This poem is a comment about the disruptions that take place in our life. When words are not enough *alludes to the beauty of contemplation and praying in a contemplative way. The thoughts here linger at the beauty of stillness and silent prayer, which brings an individual much closer to the presence of God, of feeling God's Spirit within.*

God does not send us plagues to teach us things

Some Christians seem to have a very limited image of the Holy Trinity: nasty God the Father in heaven; sweet, lovely Jesus... and the bird! While the creeds teach that there is one God in three persons, they act as one in creating, saving and inspiring. In John's Gospel Jesus says he does nothing on his own (5:30); 'the Father and I are one' (10:30); and 'to have seen me is to have seen the Father' (14:9). Christians believe that Jesus came to fulfil the Old Testament; they believe, too, that everything in the Old Testament should be interpreted through the revelation of God in Jesus Christ.

This matters when we come to understand the meaning of plagues and other natural disasters. For the peoples of the ancient world, if there was a flood, plague or pestilence then God was saying something through it. But in the Gospels Jesus never sends a plague, a natural disaster or turns anyone into a pillar of salt. If Jesus isn't into murderous retribution, neither, if we take him at his repeated word, is God the Father. Jesus is the incarnate correction to false views of how God works in the world.

So, even though Covid-19's origins are yet to be finally established, they have a natural explanation, and the way the virus has spread has been in measure the result of poor human decisions. God has not sent the pandemic upon us.

Whenever there is a local or a global catastrophe whether it is the fire that destroyed the roof of Notre Dame or the spread of Aids there are always some Christians who say that it has been sent as a punishment by God for various contemporary sins. This reveals a belief in God as a kind of extra-powerful figure ruling the universe, a chief executive who tolerates bad behaviour up to a point, but then his patience snaps and he stops the nonsense, sending a tsunami or a pandemic to remind us who is boss.

God as a vengeful tyrant is a neat if frightening solution to the deep pain in our lives: our suffering has to come from somewhere, and perhaps it is understandable that some seek the explanation that it is sent directly by God.

But there is a huge difference between God permitting evil in our world and God perpetrating such acts upon us. The Church teaches that the first proposition is true, but not the second, although listening to some Christians talking about the coronavirus pandemic you would be forgiven for thinking it did. Because God wants us to be fully free, our world holds the possibility of our choosing evil; if it were otherwise, we would be marionettes. This is a world away from God directly causing suffering and destruction.

Just because sometimes people grow through pain and suffering, it does not mean God has sent these things as a test: rather this growth is a testament to God accompanying us through every moment, inspiring us to be in solidarity with all God's children, so that together we make the best decisions in the shadow of death and the valley of tears.

Nor does God send plagues to teach us things, though we can learn from them, and we are learning a lot right now about our delicate relationship with the created order and how poor choices made in one place can have unintended consequences in other places. We are also learning that the best response to natural disasters or health emergencies is transparency, good government, honest reporting, human ingenuity, responsible citizenship, and valuing the common good; we are also learning how extraordinarily resilient some of us are in the face of tragedy

How can I be so confident that God is not deadly by nature? Because the God revealed in Jesus Christ is not a tyrant but a lover, a God prepared to go to any lengths – even to give up his life on the cross – to save us, even though we do not deserve it. John 1:5 says, 'God is light, in him there is no darkness'. If that is true, plagues and pandemics cannot be part of an arsenal of weapons deployed by an angry God to punish us for our selfishness and greed.

Spiritual sanity in these difficult days rests in seeing that every moment of every day God does what he did on Good Friday: not intervening to prevent humanity killing Jesus, but not allowing evil and despair to have the last word. The power of amazing grace enables us to make the most of even the worst situations, to help each other in every way we can, and to let light and life have the last word. Easter Sunday is God's response to Good Friday: life out of death.

Richard Leonard, SJ
Author of *What does it all mean? A guide to living lives of faith, hope and love* (Paulist Press)

(From *The Tablet*, 22 April 2020. Reproduced *by permission of Fr Richard Leonard*)

Litany of solidarity and hope during a pandemic

For those who are sick.
For those with chronic illnesses and underlying health concerns.
For all those who are suffering.

For those who are lonely.
For those who have no one to check on them.
For families that are separated.

For those who are unemployed.
For those suffering financial hardships.
For those who face an uncertain future.

For those who are suffering from physical or emotional abuse.
For those who are disproportionally suffering because of societal structures and unjust policies.
For those who are struggling with physical or mental disabilities.
For those who are overwhelmed by anxiety and stress.

For those who are dying.
For those who have died while saving the lives of others.
For all who have lost their lives.

For those who have survived.
For those who have lost their spouses.
For children who have been orphaned.
For all those who mourn and those who comfort them.

Litany of solidarity and hope during a pandemic

For firefighters, police and emergency medical workers.
For doctors, nurses, and all health care professionals.
For those who serve in the armed forces.

For public officials.
For business leaders.
For educators.
For innovators and inventors who provide new solutions,

For peace in our city and in our world.
For renewed friendships among neighbours.
For solidarity and unity among all peoples.
For a greater appreciation and love of all humanity.

For patience and perseverance.
For calm in the midst of fear.
For the grace to overcome adversity.

For generosity of spirit.
For hope in times of despair.
For light in the darkness.

Gracious and Loving God,
You are our comforter and our hope.
Hear our prayers as we come before you.
Strengthen us in this time of need.
Inspire us to acts of solidarity and generosity
And give us hope of a brighter future.

Joseph P. Shadle,
Prayers During the Coronavirus Pandemic,
www.jesuitsources.org

The theology of pandemics

Ingmar Bergman's 1957 film *The Seventh Seal* is set in medieval Sweden, as the bubonic plague ravages the countryside. In one famous scene, a procession of zombie-like flagellants enters a village and interrupts a comic stage-show.

The townspeople are present to hear the procession's leader, a bombastic preacher who proclaims that death is coming for them all: they are full of sin – lustful and gluttonous – and the plague is God's punishment for their wicked ways.

That scene is not without historical merit: the flagellants were indeed a very real phenomenon, and with the plague, the movement grew and spread throughout Europe.

For most of us, public self-mutilation and penance is a particularly extreme and repulsive form of religious fanaticism. But in the West, we still have ways of lashing ourselves, and each other, in the face of plague, pestilence and the terror they sow; and pandemics still invariably prompt a religious explanation.

During the AIDS epidemic, we were told that God was punishing homosexuals and illicit drug users. In 1992, 36 percent of Americans admitted that AIDS might be God's punishment for sexual immorality. The interesting question is: What is the temptation to view a catastrophe like the plague as divine punishment as opposed to a brute fact of nature?

Surely at least one reason we are tempted to do so is because, if it is heavenly retribution, then the hardship still has some meaning; we still live in a world with an underlying moral structure.

Indeed, to many, the idea that such a great calamity is nothing more than a brute act of nature is far more painful to contemplate than an account by which God cares enough about us to punish us.

In case you think the coronavirus is any different, it is not. On 8 March 2020, the *Times of Israel* reported that Rabbi Meir Mazuz 'claimed the spread of the deadly coronavirus in Israel and around the world is divine retribution for gay pride parades'. By some ironic twist, the rabbi is basically in agreement with Rick Wiles, a Florida pastor who said the spread of coronavirus in synagogues is a punishment of the Jewish people.

The *Jerusalem Post* quotes Wiles as saying, 'It's spreading in Israel through the synagogues. God is spreading it in your synagogues! You are under judgment because you oppose his son, Jesus Christ. That is why you have a plague in your synagogues. Repent and believe on the name of Jesus Christ, and the plague will stop'.

The temptation to view catastrophes as divine punishment is nothing to scoff or smirk at: it is entirely legitimate to want to construct a narrative out of what has occurred – to find a pattern, to derive some meaning that redeems the suffering, hardship and death.

What is unfortunate is the tendency to point to some perceived wickedness of which others are purportedly guilty as the justification for God's wrath.

Both the rabbi and the pastor are the same: both talk like Job's notorious companions, those so-called friends of the unfortunate and innocent Job, who insist that he must be guilty, that he must have sinned for God to assail him with such fury.

Of course, at the end of the poem, God tells the companions that they were wrong: Job was right –his suffering was not punishment for any sin he had committed. Indeed, the Bible teaches that God often sees fit to test precisely those that are good and righteous. Sadly, the pastor and rabbi entirely disregard that biblical lesson.

If a pandemic is divine punishment, then in a sense we can be at peace – inasmuch as we have provided the scourge with a theodicy, that is, a justification of God's ways to people.

Whenever we are faced with human tragedy, we cannot but question how an omnibenevolent and omnipotent deity would permit so much suffering to occur. A plague sharpens the concerns that lie at the heart of the theological problem of evil – the problem of reconciling a loving God with the reality and ubiquity of human and animal suffering.

Thankfully, most religious leaders are unwilling to cast the burden of guilt on any particular group of which they may disapprove. Instead, they take a page from Job and underscore the impenetrable mystery of suffering – taking their inspiration perhaps from God's speech to Job from out of the whirlwind, where he begins with one of the famous queries of the Bible: 'Where were you when I laid the earth's foundations?' And he continues with withering sarcasm, 'Who marked off its dimensions? Surely you know!' In short, do not attempt to sound the depths of God's inscrutable purpose. For every pandemic there is a theology; by their nature, they call forth notions of guilt, sin and responsibility. It is almost as if we cannot but view them through theological categories.

Each pandemic begins with a kind of 'fall', or original sin, which we attempt to retrace with our search for 'patient zero,' the individual representing the source of the calamity, the one who kicked us out of paradise as it were.

The writers of the 2011 film *Contagion* clearly had as much in mind when they decided that their story's patient zero (played by Gwyneth Paltrow) should also be an adulteress. A pandemic also highlights an inescapable function of all significant human action – namely, that our actions always outrun our intentions. Everything we do has consequences that we never anticipated, wanted or even imagined. We like to think that we are not responsible for everything our actions may cause – but the reality is that we cannot dodge or entirely relinquish our responsibility even for those things we never intended. Perhaps like nothing else, a pandemic reveals the burden of human action, our infinite liability; indeed, our indeclinable responsibility.

There is a theology accompanying every plague because there is a very human need to make sense of such colossal suffering. That theology may take the form of a conspiracy theory, but it is a theology all the same. One example is the persistent speculation that the coronavirus originated in some kind of bio-weapons laboratory in Wuhan, China. This explanation, regardless of its lack of evidentiary merit, is a temptation because it offers us a story, which is but a secularised version of the fall.

The essential features are there: to say that human beings deliberately created the virus is to say that this pandemic is the result of human transgression; that human hubris introduced this uncontrollable element that upset the order of things. The current pandemic has left fear and death, loneliness and stagnation in its wake. We must start asking ourselves what it has all been for.

Eventually, this great tide of suffering will ebb, life will resume, the economy will reopen and pick up steam, and the coronavirus will slowly fade from our immediate view – at that point, when we think of all those many tens, perhaps hundreds, of thousands who died, alone, what will we be able to point to as their legacy? What did they die for?

Undoubtedly, many will say only that their deaths were unfortunate – all we can do to honour their sacrifice is return to life as it was, prosper and grow the economy at two percent annually. If we allow that to happen, then we will have failed, completely and utterly.

If we do not seize this crisis as a moment for transformation, then we will have lost the war. If doing so requires reviving notions of collective guilt and responsibility – including the admittedly uncomfortable view that every one of us is infinitely responsible, then so be it; as long we do not morally cop out by blaming some group as the true bearers of sin, guilt and God's heavy judgment.

A pandemic clarifies the nature of action: that with our every act we answer to each other. In that light, we have a duty to seize this public crisis as an opportunity to reframe our mutual responsibility to one another and the world.

Sam Ben Meir

Professor of philosophy and world religions
Mercy College, New York City

(Essay reproduced with the permission of Professor Sam Ben Meir)

Pope Francis shares his vision for Covid's aftermath

Pope Francis has presented 'a plan for the rising up again' of humanity in the midst of a global crisis that has brought the world's peoples and the economy to their knees. He shared it in an exclusive meditation for *Vida Nueva*, the Spanish religious weekly, in which he reflects on the coronavirus pandemic in the light of the resurrection of Jesus.

'Un plan para resuciter' ('A plan for rising up again') is the title he chose for the reflection. In it, he does not conceal his concern over the crisis caused by a pandemic that has infected more than 2 million people, caused untold deaths and wreaked havoc on the world's economy. Pope Francis says our experience today mirrors in many ways that of the disciples of Jesus after his death and burial in the tomb. Like them, 'we live surrounded by an atmosphere of pain and uncertainty,' and we ask, 'Who will roll away the stone from the tomb?'

He likens the stone that sealed the tomb of Jesus to the tombstones of the pandemic that 'threatens to bury all hope' for the elderly living in total isolation, for families who lack food and for those on the front lines who are 'exhausted and overwhelmed'.

He recalls, however, that the women who followed Jesus did not allow themselves to be paralysed by anxiety and suffering. 'They found ways to overcome every obstacle,' simply 'by being and accompanying.'

He notes that many today are following suit, including 'doctors, nurses, people stocking the supermarket shelves, cleaners, caretakers, people who transport goods, public security officials, volunteers, priests, women religious, grandparents, teachers, and so many others'.

But like the women, the pope said, they all ask: 'Who will roll away the stone?'

Francis says many are participating in the passion of Christ today, either personally or at the side of others, and he reminds everyone: 'We are not alone, the Lord goes before us on our journey, and removes the stones that paralyse us.' This is the hope that no one can take from us, the pope says.

Pope Francis says the disciples of Jesus discovered something that we are now learning: 'No one is saved alone'.

Pope Francis describes the present moment as a 'propitious time' to be open to the Spirit, who can 'inspire us with a new imagination of what is possible'.

Indeed, today, 'frontiers fall, walls crumble, and all the discourse of the fundamentalists [*integratis*] dissolve in the face of an imperceptible presence which shows the fragility of which we are made.' But, he says, 'Easter calls us and invites us to remember this other discreet and respectful, generous and reconciling presence, so as to start that new life which is given to us.'

This presence 'is the breath of the Spirit that opens horizons, sparks creativity and renews brotherhood and makes us say, "I'm present" in the face of the enormous and urgent task that awaits us'.

He describes the present moment as a 'propitious time' to be open to the Spirit, who can 'inspire us with a new imagination of what is possible'. He recalls that the Spirit does not allow itself 'to be closed in or manipulated by fixed or outmoded methods or decadent structures' but rather moves us to 'make new things'.

At this moment in history, Francis says, 'We have recognised the importance of joining the entire human family in the search for a sustainable and integral development'. We have also understood that 'for better or worse all our actions affect others because everything is connected in our common home, and if the health authorities order that we remain confined in our home, it is the people who make this possible, aware of their co-responsibility in stopping the pandemic'.

He insists that 'an emergency like Covid-19 is overcome in the first place by the antibodies of solidarity'. This lesson 'breaks all the fatalism in which we have immersed ourselves and allows us to return to be the architects and protagonists of a common history,' he says, and it enables us 'to respond together to the many evils that are affecting so many of our brothers and sisters across the globe'.

'We cannot allow ourselves to write the present and future history by turning our backs on the suffering of so many people', he says. Quoting the book of Genesis, he writes that God himself is asking us, 'Where is your brother?' He expressed the hope that our response would be marked by 'hope, faith and charity'. Indeed, he says, 'if we act as one people, also in the face of the other epidemics that are hitting us, then we can have a real impact'.

In reference to these other epidemics, Francis raises a series of questions: 'Are we capable of acting responsibly in the face of the hunger, suffered by so many in a world where there is in fact food for all? Will we continue looking the other way in the face of wars fuelled by [the quest for] domination and power? Are we willing to change our style of life that submerges so many in poverty, by promoting and encouraging a more austere and human lifestyle that makes possible a more equitable sharing of resources? Will we adopt, as an international community, the necessary measures to stop the devastation of the environment, or will we continue to deny the evidence [of this devastation]? Will the globalisation of indifference continue threatening and tempting our journey?'

Pope Francis expresses the hope that, in the light of the resurrection, 'we would encounter the necessary antibodies of justice, charity and solidarity' to change the world. He calls for the building of 'a civilisation of love', which he described as 'a civilisation of hope', contrary to one marked by 'anguish and fear, sadness and discouragement, passivity and tiredness'.

This civilisation 'has to be built daily' and requires 'the commitment of everyone'.

Gerard O'Connell,
America, The Jesuit Review, 17 April 2020
(*Used with permission of the editor, America.*)

What am I to say?

> As for mortals, their days are like grass;
> They flourish like a flower of the field.
> for the wind passes over it, and it is gone;
> and its place knows it no more.
>
> Psalm 103:15–16

My friend David Baer and I recently wrote a piece in which we suggested that our current crises present an opportunity for theologians to reconsider how they speak to a world they hope might be paying some attention. We counselled theologians to abandon the offices of pundit and scold: in our opinion, theology has more than finger-wagging and 'takes' to offer. Though the temptations of scolding are difficult to resist, and punditry by definition finds a ready audience, theologians can take consolation in knowing their job well done involves turning their hearers' eyes toward God, even if only for a moment. In this piece, I speak to my colleagues, to the theologians and academics who find themselves seduced by easy forays into topical and timely speech.

Within Catholicism, the language of the 'signs of the times' has been a popular and sometimes effective means of signalling the intention of theologians to speak meaningfully to their communities. We theologians use the language of the signs of the times as a mechanism by which to try and locate—and compete about—this or that social phenomenon deserving special attention. It typically ranges across a spectrum of political and social issues (poverty and inequality, immigration, abortion, gay marriage, this or that sense of social 'progress' or decline, and so on). The power of invoking the signs of the times consists in attaching gospel language to important social concerns. Its weakness, however, is built into that strength. By attaching the gospel to contemporary concerns theologians can lose sight of that horizon toward which Jesus directed his disciples. The horizon of the signs of the times is the end of the age (Matthew 24:3). 'See to it that you are not alarmed', Jesus counsels the disciples: do not be misled by false messiahs or become alarmed by events. Stand firm, he tells them, because they know the events point to his return.

That horizon has too often been discounted even by those who should know better. And thus our communal conversation, a conversation among Catholics that should be open enough even to include all those Christians and non-Christians who believe in a Creator, parrots the conversation of our age in its lack of discipline, honesty, and graciousness. Instead of reflecting the community and its capacity for extra-ecclesial openness, the conversation is closed even to those in the communion of the church. In tone and approach, the voices are preening and finger-wagging and virtue-signalling.

This has become most evident in the responses of the church and its spokespeople (of which I am one) during our various crises: COVID-19, lockdown, the new confrontation with racial bias, the riots, the protests. Rather than follow the disciplined practice of looking at current events against a theological horizon common to the greatest sermons handed down to us, theologians and others have weighed in on masks and re openings and epidemiological interpretations. In some cases, with a nearly perverse sense of pleasure, they have noted how events confirm their own ways of seeing the world. All of that is good sport, especially in the Twitter shit hole. But none of that builds a solid structure of understanding, and almost all of it is absorbed into the white noise of a culture in desperate need of distinct, clear counsel.

During these crises, we have witnessed the weighing up of seemingly opposed alternatives: lives or the economy, law and order or justice. Reasonable cases have been made on all sides of the weight of the one against the other. As Christians, however, we know the impoverishment of this approach. Lives are always at stake. All of our lives are lived against the backdrop of mortality. Order or justice? Justice is an expression of order; disorder can never be justice, and yet the justice we enjoy is always mixed and partial and fragile. The choices we face are not between 'lives or the economy', or 'justice or order', but between, as Augustine says in a sermon, 'begging in this world, and reigning with Christ'. We so love life, many would beggar themselves for just another day, a few more hours, a last moment; how many, Augustine wonders, recognise they are only delaying death at the cost of eternal life? We are like blades of grass, the psalmist says, soon enough windswept and forgotten even by the place we once stood.

> Silence is a space, and silence can be fertile. Without the patience to allow that seed of the Word to grow, our thinking becomes barren.

'What am I to say?' Augustine asks in the same sermon. What words, what threats, can a world-historical rhetorician employ to melt the 'ice of earthly numbness' of his hearers who continue to so love life they would beggar themselves at the cost of eternal happiness? That question is ours.

I don't know what to say either. Augustine was stupefied at the prospects of breaking through the numbness of his hearers, and yet he spoke, sowing the seed of the word. A speaker of such great gifts, he recognised the needs of his community and spoke from those gifts, to those far beyond his time and place. Today, speakers of louder voices and fewer gifts are holding forth, echoing, too often, both sides of the terms of the debate that are set by those without the horizon of the resurrection. The noise of the surety of our colleagues and friends, of sudden expertise, is pummelling our ears, drowning out the silence that we need to hear the word of God. Silence is a space, and silence can be fertile. Without the patience to allow that seed of the Word to grow, our thinking becomes barren.

Today, I wonder if perhaps the greatest gift of many of us might be to answer Augustine's question with this: 'For now, I do not know'. We can continue to say the things that are unshakenly true. We can continue to do our work. For the rest, we can be attentive for wisdom, and while we wait in the not knowing, we can let the sliver of silence and peaceful uncertainty we offer be a gift to a world that needs fewer takes and more quiet.

Joseph Capizzi
Ordinary Professor of Moral Theology,
Catholic University of America.

(*Article reproduced by permission of the author*)

Part 2

The love, power and prophetic voice of Christian mystics

The love and power of Christian mystics: ancient and modern

The word 'mysticism' provokes prejudice among certain Christians. Historically, many of those within the Church had an element of mystery in their life. Some of these people eventually were declared saints. Others were well known artists, writers, priests, poets, or those possessing deep creativity.

Throughout Christian history, many had an element of mysticism in their life, at times expressed in their writings. The people who are mentioned in the following pages showed by their life and teaching that they embodied great goodness and love. Their lives illustrated that they lived in close communion with the Lord. They embody a power, a love, a deep spiritual longing in the totality of their lives. Much of what they said and wrote showed everlasting truth, truly biblical, as well as sacramental and a saintliness in their lifestyle. They helped others and their life and work continues to help us now.

How they lived and what they taught displayed charity, kindness and concern for their fellow human beings. Their lives invigorated the Church as they dedicated themselves and showed through their teaching and practice how to live as disciples of God. Augustine, Francis of Assisi, Julian of Norwich, Teresa of Avila and John of the Cross were only a few among many who left messages of faith, hope and love.

The extracts in this section illustrate the virtues of these people who left their mark on Christian history.

Early Christian saints, as well as those from Medieval and Renaissance times, have been declared as mystics. A mystic is someone who knows God, who incorporates the presence of God and whose life embodies love. In the modern era people such as Thomas Merton, Henri Nouwen and Richard Rohr are included. Their lives and teaching grant us an insight of how to live more fully, irrespective of our material circumstances.

At a time of the ongoing global COVID pandemic when society is in the process of transformation, it is useful to look, even briefly, at the way these people found God. They 'located their wounds' and their lives became a witness to the worldwide Church.

The mystics illustrated within these pages teach us how to find God. They represent only a few people, a scattering of 'saints and sinners' in the lengthy road of Christian history. As the famous Jesuit priest and scholar, Karl Rahner, once said, 'We all need to discover the mystical heartbeat that lies at the centre of our spiritual life and continue to live this life within our souls'.

In other words, a mystical way of looking at the world is not deviating from the Church; rather, this way of thinking and acting is, in itself, God's gift, available to all. The mystics outlined here are like guides to us in this broken and sick world which has been enveloped in a historical global viral crisis. Even the wonder and technology of modern medicine has difficulty in containing this world-wide plague.

> You have made us for yourself, O Lord,
> and our hearts are restless
> until they rest in you.
> Augustine, *Confessions*, 1.1.1.

'Our hearts are restless until they rest in you.'

These are powerful words. They direct us toward Christ in a simple way that speaks for everyone, for everyone has a restless heart. Pope Francis tells us that Augustine is speaking of three types of restlessness: 'the restlessness of spiritual seeking, the restlessness of the encounter with God, the restlessness of love'. This restlessness, whether we recognise it or not, is a desire to know God and to have a deeper relationship with him. None of this is easy, but God is always there for us. He is waiting with open arms, just as he waited for Augustine in his conversion to accepting Christ.

Of course, the natural question to ask is how we can rest in the Lord. Augustine gives us a clear answer in his *Confessions*. He says:

> No-one knows what they themselves are made of, except their own spirit within them, yet there is still some part of them that remains hidden even from their own spirit, but you, Lord, know everything about human beings because you have made them... Let me, them confess what I know about myself and confess too what I do not know, because what I know of myself I know only because you shed light on me, and what I do not know I shall remain ignorant about until my darkness becomes like bright noon before your face. (Book 1).

Augustine gives us an important model of faith to follow, one of deep personal reflection, one that teaches us how to reflect and why we should reflect. Why? Because in reflection, we find God. Augustine is very clear about how reflection works. He says, 'What I know of myself I know only because you shed light on me'. Reflection is not solitary: we have to reflect *with* God. It is a prayer. We have all been told that prayer is an integral aspect of our everyday lives, but prayer does not need to be formulaic. It does not always have to be recited from the back of a card. These types of prayers are amazing and helpful in directing our lives, but some of the most beautiful prayer is when we reflect with God, when we open up ourselves to him and just talk to him and listen to him in our hearts.

Who better to show us the importance of reflection than Mary, our Mother? In the gospel of Luke, we are told: 'His mother treasured all these things in her heart'. Mary, the Mother of God, born without sin, who through her body brought Jesus into the world, still took the time to reflect *with* the Lord.

Both Augustine and Mary are powerful examples to us. They were holy people, but they were also humans, with their weaknesses. They faced struggles, happiness and sadness in their lives. Their hearts were restless in their journeys toward the Lord.

Paul Kraus

Christ the physician

A reflection by Augustine of Hippo on the story of the two blind men sitting by the side of the road and crying out 'Lord, have mercy on is, Son of David'. (Matthew 20:30)

You know that our Lord and Saviour Jesus Christ is the physician of our eternal health, and that to this end he took on the weakness of our nature, that our weakness might not last forever. For he assumed a mortal body, wherein to kill death. And though he was crucified through weakness, as the apostle says, yet he lives by the power of God. They are the words too of the same apostle: 'He dies no more, and death shall have no more dominion over him'.

These things, I say, are well known to your faith. And there is also this which follows from it: that we should know that all the miracles which he did on the body avail to our instruction, that we may from them perceive that which is not to pass away, nor to have any end. He restored to the blind those eyes which death was sure sometime to close; he raised Lazarus to life who was to die again. And whatever he did for the health of bodies, he did it not that they should be forever; whereas at the last he will give eternal health even to the body itself. But because those things which were not seen, were not believed; by means of these temporal things which were seen, he built up faith in those things which were not seen.

These things, then, the Lord did to invite us to the faith. This faith reigns now in the church, which is spread throughout the whole world. And now he works greater cures, on account of which he did not disdain to exhibit those lesser ones. The physician gave us precepts when we were whole, that we might not need a physician. They that are whole, he says, need not a physician, but they that are sick. When whole, we despised these precepts, and by experience have felt how to our own destruction we despised his precepts. Now we are sick, we are in distress, we are on the bed of weakness, yet let us not despair. For because we could not come to the physician, he has vouchsafed to come to us himself.

Come. His house is not too narrow for you; the kingdom of God is possessed equally by all and wholly by each one; it is not diminished by the increasing number of those who possess it, because it is not divided. And that which is possessed by many with one heart is whole and entire for each one.

Augustine of Hippo, 'Sermon 38 on the New Testament' in *Nicene and Post- Nicene Fathers*, First Series, Vol. 6, ed. Philip Schaff, trans. R. G. MacMullen (T & T Clark, 1980.) Open Book of Religion review website.

What can St Augustine teach us about living through a pandemic?

In the last years of St Augustine's life, in the early fifth century, he watched as Germanic vandals marched across northern Africa, pillaging and occupying cities along the way until finally besieging his own city of Hippo. To-day, as we watch Covid-19 make its way across the globe, ravaging nations and instilling fear, we can learn much from his insights. Though Augustine might seem an unlikely source of hope (given his reputation for pessimism), his spirituality can offer inspiration and guidance at this time.

Augustine's political ethic is based on scepticism about the intentions of political authority and the pursuit of power, but he maintains that the rule of law is critical to the formation of a just society: 'Many people are benefited by being compelled in the first place through fear... so that subsequently they are able to be taught, and then pursue in action what they have learnt in words.... However, just as [people] guided by love are better, so [people] reformed by fear are more numerous'.

As we consider the stay-at-home orders intended to preserve the health of the most vulnerable among us, Christians should lead the effort to adhere to them out of love for our neighbours. Perhaps if we were willing to maintain social distance voluntarily, the authorities would not need to be so intrusive. Nevertheless, even those who protest the orders should not ignore the recommendations of public health officials. They should not tempt the Lord 'by expecting divine miraculous interposition on every occasion'.

Augustine does not encourage unnecessary physical risk as a form of faith or devotion; complete disregard for one's physical health is incompatible with his ethics. While Augustine prioritises spiritual well-being and recognises that there may be circumstances when it requires the sacrifice of physical security, he affirms that physical health is a part of the whole of human flourishing. Our bodies are goods to be protected, so long as we 'do much good with them, but no evil for their sake'. We are misguided if we place ourselves in unnecessary danger even for spiritual goods. We see this, for example, in Augustine's recommendation that fasting should be practised 'as you are able without impairing your physical health'. Notably, during the military siege of Hippo, Augustine declined to send letters advising a friend on spiritual matters because he was concerned about the physical risk to the letter bearer.

Relatedly, our social distancing must not be self-centred. While it can be easy to fall into an individualistic mentality and focus only on our personal struggles, we must expand our horizons of concern. For Augustine, spiritual health requires serving others. Augustine's *Homilies on the First Letter of John* reflect on John's insight that love does not abide in anyone who closes his or her heart to those in need. Taking Christ's self-sacrifice to be the essence of love, Augustine exhorts us to 'see where love begins. If you're not yet capable of dying for your sister or brother, be capable even now of giving him [or her] some of your goods. Let love stir your heart to action now'.

In other words, while perfect self-sacrificial love might be difficult for us, there are ways to nurture its seed: 'Give of your temporal abundance to free a sister or brother from temporal distress. This is where love starts'. For Augustine, everything we do is a result of our love a pursuit of what we desire. Ensuring that our love is formed properly that we value others rightly, in light of their participation in the broader whole is critical for the pursuit of justice. By serving others in need, we can develop this love that 'has been poured out into our hearts by the Holy Spirit'.

During this pandemic, the opportunities to serve are many, and it is incumbent upon us to pursue them. From donating to organisations on the front lines of this crisis to reaching out to neighbors in need of groceries or emotional support, we should be finding ways to serve focusing particularly on those who are especially vulnerable due to age, race, class or legal status. It should be noted that this is incumbent upon all of us to the extent that we are able: We all have something to share; but of those more privileged, more is required. This point, however, should not be misconstrued to encourage the elderly to give their lives for the sake of the economy because there are certainly other, less dangerous, means of preserving our society's economic health.

Finally, because all action stems from love in Augustine's view, our political structures will be good or bad to the extent that they are developed by persons with rightly ordered or malformed love. The pandemic has exposed structural injustices that are not only morally repugnant but detrimental to public health – racial and economic divisions, health care inequality, reticence toward environmental protection measures and the criminalisation of migration come readily to mind. Augustine advocates for the protection of 'a life of bodily health [and] the means of staying alive' for all people. He emphasises equality, maintaining that no one should 'say that he [or she] is more worthy of life than others'.

If we are to practise love, then, we must strive, to the best of our ability, to develop systems and enact policies that advance the common good and promote the full dignity and participation of all an elusive goal, perhaps, but one that nevertheless demands our unceasing effort.

The slowness of life for many of us now provides the opportunity to reflect on these issues. Indeed, Augustine's spirituality is centered on the interplay of contemplation and action. Augustine maintains that when we love God, we will spend time in contemplation, and the delight we find in this contemplation will compel us to undertake 'righteous engagement in affairs'. He writes, 'No one ought to be so leisured as to take no thought in that leisure for the interest of [one's] neighbour, nor so active as to feel no need for the contemplation of God'.

During this pandemic, we should embrace the slowness of life and refill our spiritual reservoir but doing so should compel us into the heart of the world to act for justice. We should take this time before the reopening of our society to improve our physical and spiritual health, nurture the seed of love, and begin to develop ways to advocate for change. Augustine's recollection of a period of grief in his own life is encouraging: 'Time never stands still, nor does it idly pass without effect upon our feelings or fail to work its wonders on the mind. It came and went, day after day, and as it passed it filled me with fresh hope and new thoughts to remember. Little by little it pieced me together again'. This pandemic could be the start of something beautiful if we resolve through grace to make it so.

Kathleen Bonnette, 28 May 2020

(Reprinted from *America, The Jesuit Review*, with permission of the editor.)

Our life, our hope, our healing

We believe that where people are gathered together in love God is present and good things happen: life is full.

We believe that we are immersed in mystery... that our lives are more than they seem... that we belong to each other...

And to a universe of great creative energies whose source and destiny is God.

We believe that God is after us... that he is calling us from the depth of human life.

We believe that God has risked himself and become man in Jesus and with Jesus we believe that each of us is situated in the love of God...

The pattern of our life will be the pattern of Jesus through death... to resurrection.

And most deeply we believe that in our struggle to love we incarnate God in the world.

And so aware of mystery and wonder, caught in friendship and laughter we become speechless before the joy in our hearts and celebrate the sacredness of life in the Eucharist.

Source unknown

Julian of Norwich: the plague and the pandemic

Most of us who have lived within the last hundred years have been taken by surprise by the Covid-19 pandemic that spread across the globe in 2020. While those of us in the western world may have been aware of SARS, MERS and EBOLA and had a historical understanding of the Spanish Flu of 1918, we have not lived in fear that a pandemic could totally upend society in the way it has. The economic and social implications are massive and while governments have attempted to cushion the impacts, the results have been great suffering, death and dislocation. Much has been written about the transformative effects of lock-down and some of the beneficial changes that have resulted from a slower pace of life.

In an attempt to understand the positive benefits of a life of isolation, it can be helpful to study the writings of the fourteenth century mystic known as Julian of Norwich. She was born in the city of Norwich in 1343 and survived the Black Death at the age of five, as well as the bubonic plague in 1355. About one third of England's population may have succumbed to this illness which not only ravaged England but most of Europe.

How and why are Julian's writings relevant to our time? She authored the *Revelation of Divine Love* and the *Showings* that speak much about the response to suffering in a world that is torn apart by dislocation. Her writings and visions relate directly to her experience surviving multiple outbreaks of the plague, show a direction towards an abiding state of peace that surpasses the awful undercurrents of any illness or pandemic. God's redemption, forgiveness and wholeness through suffering is one of the overriding themes of Julian's writing.

Prayer and prudent action go hand in hand, as well as a trust in God's promises. In one sense, Julian's writings illustrated the promises St Paul made in his letter to the Romans (Romans 8:38-39): 'I am convinced that neither death, nor life, nor angels, nor rulers, nor things present, nor things to come, nor powers, nor height, nor depth, nor anything else in all creation, will be able to separate us from the love of God in Christ Jesus'. Life was difficult in the fourteenth century world of Julian of Norwich. Plague, death and social upheaval characterised the ordinary person's life.

Despite the harrowing circumstances of life at that time, Julian of Norwich, in her revelation and writings, knew that God would redeem all those whose trust was in him. God would bring to wholeness and grant everlasting life to those whose faith was in Christ Jesus.

Julian chose the solitary life of the mystic where she spent years in silence praying for those around her. She wrote of Christ's great love for us, as well as the joy and hope his followers can enjoy. She also wrote in some detail about that wonderful Christian word 'hope'. Jesus was the great hope for all in every age.

Finally, Julian's life was deeply prayerful. Prayer was wholeheartedly integrated into her life, which was lived as a silent mystic. Her writing showed that prayer was a great act of trust. Following her example, we can pray for regeneration and revival in our broken world and for a restoration of God-given values.

Paul Kraus

Julian of Norwich speaks about our earth

'I was wholly at peace, at ease and at rest, so that there was nothing upon the earth which could have afflicted me. This lasted for a time, and then I was changed... I felt there was no ease or comfort for me except faith, hope and love, and truly I felt very little of this. And then presently God gave me again comfort and rest for my soul... and the again I felt the pain, and then afterwards the delight and joy, now the one and now the other, again and again, I suppose twenty times.'

'If any such lover be in earth which is continually kept from falling, I know it not: for it was not shewed me. But this was shewed: that in falling and in raising we are ever preciously kept in love.'

'The love that made him to suffer passeth as far all his pains as Heaven is above Earth.'

'We may never come to full knowing of God till we know first clearly our own soul.'

'All shall be well, all shall be well, all shall be well... For there is a Force of love moving through the universe that holds us fast and will never let us go.'

Perhaps the best answer to the question 'Why Julian now?' is that in our age of uncertainty, inconceivable suffering, and seemingly perpetual violence and war... Julian shows us the way toward contemplative peace.

> Excerpts from Veronica Mary Rolf, *An Explorer's Guide To Julian of Norwich*, IVP Academic, 2018.
>
> (From: *Explorer's Guides, Reading Religion*, A Publication of the American Academy of Religion - a website open book review.)

Stillness, silence...

We need silence to be able to touch our souls... to be able to hear ourselves... God is the friend of silence.

Mother Teresa

An embroidered sky...
Three dimensional

tapestry: glorious
golden beams

stream in between
gracious clouds as

the luminance of the rainbow
speaks in a lyrical voice.

A healing silence
in soothing stillness

like a prophet's voice
from the distant past

who contemplates
this grandness.

Lucent colours
illuminate, identify

moments with no time,
in still, perfect peace,

serenity in this quietude.
Therapy of mind and spirit.

A wellness of wonder,
almost holiness

captures a brief
unfolding moment

of great splendour.
An infinite surrender

of unending time,
eternal space.

Paul Kraus

A prayer for those suffering from the coronavirus

*You will not fear the terror of the night
or the arrow that flies by day,
or the pestilence that stalks in darkness,
or the destruction that wastes at noonday.*

Psalm 91:5-6

Merciful God, hear our fervent prayer
for all who suffer from the coronavirus.
May those who are infected receive the proper treatment
and the comfort of your healing presence.
May their caregivers, families and neighbours be shielded
from the onslaught of the virus.
Give solace to those who grieve the loss of loved ones.
Protect and guide those who strive to find a cure,
that their work may conquer the disease
and restore communities to wholeness and health.
Help us to rise above fear.

We ask all this through the name of your Son, Jesus, and the Holy Spirit, now and forever.

Amen.

This prayer is taken from the *Catholic Health Association of America.*)

Peace prayer of St Francis

For more than the past century and throughout the western world, the following words have been regarded as a 'classic' prayer.

The prayer is actually a pathway of peace. It suggests great hope and healing for any life. We are encouraged in the gospel of St Matthew to 'let our light shine before others, so that they may see good deeds and glorify your Father in heaven'. This prayer shows us how we can gain a feeling of overall peace. It is uplifting, encouraging and brings a sense of holiness all of us are able to achieve.

Lord, make me an instrument of your peace:
where there is hatred, let me sow love;
where there is injury, pardon;
where there is doubt, faith;
where there is despair, hope;
where there is darkness, light;
where there is sadness, joy.

O divine Master, grant that I may not so much seek
to be consoled as to console,
to be understood as to understand,
to be loved as to love.
For it is in giving that we receive,
it is in pardoning that we are pardoned,
and it is in dying that we are born to eternal life.
Amen.

Fr Esther Bouquerel (1855-1923)

A Franciscan benediction

May God bless you with discomfort
At easy answers, half-truths, and superficial relationships
So that you may live deep within your heart.

May God bless you with anger
At injustice, oppressions, and exploitation of people,
So that you may work for justice, freedom and peace.

May God bless you with tears
To shed for those who suffer pain, rejection, hunger and war,
So that you may reach out your hand to comfort them and
Turn their pain into joy.

And may God bless you with enough foolishness
To believe that you can make a difference in the world,
So that you can do what others claim cannot be done
To bring justice and kindness to all our children and the poor.

Richard Rohr

Teresa of Avila and John of the Cross

St Teresa (1515-1582) was a Spanish Carmelite nun who came from the noble class and entered the convent slightly against the wishes of her family. She is remembered primarily as a person whose writings convey the love of God in Jesus, as well as peace with God. She is also remembered as a theologian, a mystic and a religious reformer who emphasised contemplative prayer. She powerfully influenced a much younger Carmelite friar and mystic, John of the Cross, whose poetic writings were voluminous and whose writing also had deep spiritual significance within the church and far beyond. St Teresa taught us that prayer is about relationship and that we are never alone when we pray.

Teresa and John of the Cross wrote about the love of Christ, the 'Night of the Soul' increasing as our life journey proceeds. Her writings repeatedly mentioned that God stays with us throughout life and his Spirit enables us through thick and thin.

Suffering and death are normative aspects of our inner world, but the ultimate reality is the resurrection, our new birth, that can take place as a result of Christ's atonement on the cross. This truth pervades the writing of both Teresa and John of the Cross. They both lived through the beginning of the split within the Church that resulted in the Reformation in Europe. Teresa's writing contains not only deep spirituality but points us to inner peace as a result. This is similar to the profound meanings found within the writing of John of the Cross.

With the contemporary world having been plunged into economic, social, religious and political dislocation, also with the apparent retreat from true democracy across a number of nations, as well as the 'conspiracy theory' regarding the advent of this virus from China, peace at any level has been put into peril. The worldwide statistics of the COVID virus pandemic are alarming and still seem to be making news.

Countless numbers worldwide have been hospitalised, endless people have lost their means of employment in a number of nations across the world. In Europe and across the United States, the death toll has caused great suffering. Dislocation at every level of society has been like the virus itself and has changed the priorities of so many nations.

The fact that churches across the world have closed their doors implies that the very culture of religious belief has changed. The power and structure of the church is in focus. The encouraging and direct words of Pope Francis in his latest encyclical, Fratelli Tutti, on fraternity and social friendship within the church form a reminder of how the church, the people of God, should witness in this spiritually lost world in which we live.

How is the church evangelising in this world that has been shaken to its roots by insecurity and loss? In a number of ways, including the great hunger to participate at a personal level in the liturgy and for the laity to be more involved in the corporate leadership of the church.

The faith of individuals in this age of economic recession and the ever increasing numbers of unemployed has also turned people to wonder how God still loves them and is relevant to their needs.

The writings of Teresa of Avila and John of the Cross speak to us, individually and corporately. The following quotes from a poem by St. Teresa mirror words from St Paul about a 'peace that passes all understanding'.

> 'Let nothing disturb you, nothing frighten you. All things pass away. God alone is changeless. Patience achieves all things. Who has God, lacks nothing. God alone is sufficient.'

This poem almost echoes a response to the dislocation and hurt experienced in our world at the time of this coronavirus pandemic. Countless people suffer through poor health, commercial dislocation, unemployment and social isolation, as well as a state of helplessness. Innocent lives are hurt wherever one looks in the world.

'The feeling remains that God is on the journey, too.'

When adverse circumstances confront us on our life's journey, when fear, suffering, especially illness or loss of job, home, or some other evil circumstance gives us a devastating emotional or physical blow, we need to look at the meaning of the Cross, to consider God's great love for each of us by atoning our weakness and granting us eternal life. Only then can we realise that God, in the humanity of Jesus, the everlasting Christ, still walks with us. Thinking and believing this will bring us peace, faith and hope that no material circumstance, can take away from us.

'Today, may there be peace within. May you trust God that you are exactly where you are meant to be. May you not forget the infinite possibilities that are born of faith. May you use those gifts that you

have received, and pass on the love that has been given to you. May you be content, knowing you are a child of God. Let this presence settle into your bones, and allow your soul the freedom to sing, dance, praise and love. It is there for each and every one of us.'

Especially in the disruption we face, in our stress and anxiety, we can easily lose sight of our own purpose, our direction in life and our peace of mind. Pain and suffering may last for far longer than we could have imagined. Yet, over and above, beyond our pain, we are assured of being God's children. Our earthly life is rather fleeting and we pray for a faith that overcomes this so-called violence within our life. The waywardness of our circumstance is passing, yet beneath and beyond this suffering, God loves us, a love that will last forever.

'Christ has no body now, but yours. No hands, no feet on earth, but yours. Yours are the eyes through which Christ looks compassion into the world. Yours are the feet which Christ walks to do good. Yours are the hands with which Christ blesses the world.'

These words might almost seem to be an irony in this world which is bathed in the suffering of the COVID pandemic. Even within the wealthy nations, especially throughout the United States, the number of unemployed, sick and disadvantaged is growing. Stability is something that has lost its meaning for those who believed that life had been safe and predictable. Helplessness has yet again overcome people who had, to some degree, felt secure. Yet these words from St Teresa remind us that peacefulness is planted by Christ himself: peace that only seeks goodness and love which was ultimately expressed in the death of the Lord Jesus. We can live either with a sense of belonging or a sense of isolation. These words have always been powerful reminders of being loved by Jesus, our living Christ.

St Teresa of Avila wrote extensively on life, spirituality and suffering for about forty years. Her main works include *The Way of Perfection* (1583), *The Interior Castle* (1588) and *Spiritual Relations, Exclamations of the Soul to God* (1588). Teresa suffered from poor health yet she demonstrated in her writing that suffering enhances spiritual growth because we learn to surrender ourselves to Almighty God and we also learn to rise above sickness and health, especially by the fact that God transcends our suffering and ultimately will bless us with everlasting life. Through these works, Teresa repeatedly teaches that death is certainly not the 'be all and end all' and that faith, hope and courage overcome suffering. She lived during the time of the Spanish Inquisition, a time of persecution, particularly to that unfortunate minority who were the Jews. Her life overlapped with Ignatius of Loyola, founder of the Jesuits, and, as already explained, John of the Cross. Her mystical mind found powerful expression in her writing, whose focus was to teach her readers about the real power of prayer. Prayer is about relationship, a theme that repeatedly emerges in her major works. Her recurring theme is that God is forever with us when we pray. She was canonised as a saint in the Catholic Church in 1622, fifty years after her death. In 1970, Pope Paul V1 declared her a Doctor of the Church, meaning that her writings bear true standing within the sanctity of the Church.

Paul Kraus

St John of the Cross

Like Teresa of Avila, John was also a Spaniard who lived from 1542 to 1591. He was born into a poor family and like Teresa of Avila, entered the Carmelite Order in 1563. He took the name of John of St Matthias. In 1567, he was ordained a priest and not long after met Teresa of Avila. In a rather complicated life in the first years of his priesthood, and for a few years from 1577, he became a prisoner for instigating reforms in a Carmelite monastery. He spent much time in solitary confinement until he escaped from this situation in 1580 and began a new Order called the Discalced Carmelites.

From that time, he worked as a religious reformer. During his imprisonment he wrote many poems which reflect the beauty of a Christian mystic. He also wrote four books, including a famous poem, *Dark Night of the Soul*, which was a commentary on inner purification. The narrative of this work is full of beautiful images which compares the 'darkness of the human soul', the darkness of being purified, with the mystical love that comes from God. He also wrote of contemplative prayer and its true humility. Finally, in this brief commentary, he pointed to the love of God which abandons oneself and makes one selfless. John of the Cross wrote regularly of the 'nearness of God', who is 'more near to us than we are to ourselves'.

The following biblical texts are a summary of this great poet and reformer of our faith at a turbulent time in the history of Spain, his native land:

'*For we walk by faith, and not by sight.*' (2 Corinthians 5:7)

'*If any want to become my followers, let them deny themselves and take up their cross daily and follow me.*' (Luke 9:23)

Other texts from John of the Cross

'The soul that walks in love neither tires others nor grows tired ... In the dark night of the soul, bright flows the river of God... In the twilight of life, God will not judge us on our early possessions and human success, but rather on how much we loved.' (*The Dark Night of the Soul.*)

'Strive to preserve your heart in peace; let no event of this world disturb it.'

'The endurance of darkness is the preparation for great light.'

'In tribulation, immediately draw near to God with confidence, and you will receive strength, enlightenment and instruction.'

'Contemplation is nothing else but a secret, peaceful and loving infusion of God, which if admitted, will set the soul on fire with the Spirit of love.'

'In order to come to union with the wisdom of God, the soul has to proceed by unknowing rather than by knowing.'

'And in its substance the soul suffers profoundly from its poverty and abandonment... the soul must needs suffer the purgation and remedy, according to the nature of its sickness...'

(Selections from *The Poems of St. John of the Cross*, translated by Willis Barnstone, New York, New Directions, 1972. These extracts are taken from the internet source: Springer Link, Palgrave Literature Collection.)

A statement about John of the Cross by John Paul II said: 'The spiritual journey is totally sustained by grace, which none the less demands an intense spiritual commitment and is no stranger to painful purifications (the "dark night"). But it leads in various possible ways, to the ineffable joy experienced by the mystics as a 'nuptila' union. Examples of this ineffable joy are the teachings of Saint John of the Cross and Saint Teresa of Avila.' (*Novo Millennio Inuente*.)

Dark Night of the Soul

On a dark night,
Kindled in love with yearnings – oh, happy chance! –
I went forth without being observed,
My house being now at rest.

In darkness and secure,
By the secret ladder, disguised – oh, happy dance! –
In darkness and in concealment,
My house being now at rest.

In the happy night,
In secret, when none saw me,
Nor I beheld aught,
Without light or guide, save that which burned in my
Heart.
This light guided me
More surely than the light of noonday
To the place where he (well I knew who!) was awaiting me -
A place where none appeared.

Oh, night that guided me,
Oh, night more lovely than the dawn,
Oh might that joined Beloved with lover,
Lover transformed in the Beloved!

Upon my flowery breast,
Kept wholly for himself alone,
There he stayed sleeping, and I caressed him,
And the inning of the cedars made a breeze.

The breeze blew from the turret
As I parted his locks;
With his gentle hand he wounded my neck
And used all my senses to be suspended.

I remained, lost in oblivion;
My face I reclined on the Beloved.
All ceased and I abandoned myself myself,
Leaving my cares forgotten among the lilies.

    The term 'dark night of the soul' in Catholic spirituality describes a spiritual crisis in the journey toward union with God, like that described here in this poem by St. John of the Cross. This spiritual crisis might be temporary or it might endure for a long time. Just as people across the globe have found the effects of COVID-19 has disrupted their lifestyle by sadness, frustration, hopelessness or other hardship, we find in this poem answers that might reinstate hope and faith to those in difficulty. The 'light and guide' includes being informed, surrendering oneself to the power of God, especially in the form of prayer and meditation, giving and receiving kindness and love and living in the present, not in the past or the future. This poem has endured for centuries because it points to the love, power and hope God grants to all who seek Him.

(Taken from 'Poet Seers' - Spiritual and Devotional Poets - The Works of St. John of the Cross - Dark Night of the Soul. Used from Internet copy)

Paul Kraus

Conversation of the heart

An icy wind of loneliness touches each of us
At times. Dignity of solitude bypasses words,
Painful, yet always pure. Loneliness,
Even solitude bring little energy to the soul.
Our hearts are restless... until they rest in you.

Stillness, silence sometimes brings healing.
Redemption comes easily in this state,
Swept away by the Spirit with strong feeling.
A spirit, gentle and sweet without any fate.
Our hearts are restless... until they rest in you.

A state of being, not a place or time.
This mindset harbours quietness,
Painful yet peaceful, always in its space.
This mode of quietness still the mind.
Our hearts are restless... until they rest in you.

We finally cry in watchful speech,
Occasionally in anguish, anger, pain.
Little bitterness, no rejection now. We're taught
The prayer of openness, not any single stain.
Our hearts are restless... until they find a rest in you.

We pray inaudible prayers of the heart, not careful
Word filled thoughts. A graceful balance
Of the mind, no priority of any kind.
This intricate mosaic of our life.
Our hearts are restless... until they rest in you.

Clarity, beauty, serenity arrives. A wholeness,
A fullness, strangely sounding to ordinary minds.
Solitude is, in a sense, our essential being.
A lovely mystery of the heart now sublime.
Our hearts are restless... until they rest in you.

Silence, soft words and peaceful harmony.
Prayer of the spirit, a healing openness
Surpassing sermons, brings hope and healing.
Sacred and secular message, achieving outspokenness.
Our hearts are restless... until they find a rest in you.

                                                  Paul Kraus

Defying the Covid pandemic

What we would like to do is change the world make it a little simpler for people to feed, clothe, and shelter themselves as God intended them to do. And to a certain extent, by fighting for better conditions, by crying out unceasingly for the rights of the workers, of the poor, of the destitute... we can to a certain extent change the world; we can work for the oasis, the little cell of joy and peace in a harried world.

> Dorothy Day, 1897-1980, Christian mystic, founder of the Catholic Worker Movement.

Let us give up our work, our thoughts, our plans, ourselves, our lives, our loved ones, our influence, our all, right into his hand, and then, when we have given all over to him, there will be nothing left for us to be troubled about, or to make trouble about.

> Hudson Taylor, 1832-1905, physician and missionary

You shall worship the Lord your God, and I will bless your bread and water; and I will take sickness away from among you.

> Exodus 23:25

Inner attitude: a barometer of our health

In recent times, it has been made abundantly clear that we are not quite as 'free' in our society as we may have thought. While we understand that the laws passed by government are designed to protect us, we may feel resentful at being kept from family and work or being forced to wear a mask.

While changing our circumstances may be difficult, or even impossible, our attitude to adversity has a powerful effect on the outcome. So much depends on our attitude to the outcome that it can have a profound effect on our physical and mental health.

A healthy relationship of body, mind and spirit creating a balanced lifestyle results in the ability to manage stress and therefore mitigate many physical illnesses. Numerous passages of Scripture confirm this truth as is shown in the book of Jeremiah:

'The heart is devious above all else; it is perverse who can understand it? I the Lord test the mind and search the heart, to give to all according to their ways, according to the fruit of their doings.' (Jeremiah 17:9-10)

'A cheerful heart is a good medicine, but a downcast spirit dries up the bones.' (Proverbs 17:22)

Jesus himself reinforced many of the quotes from Proverbs when some of his healing miracles linked physical and emotional healing. When Jesus healed the man who was paralysed, he also released that man from a burdened conscience: 'Take heart... your sins are forgiven' (Matthew 9:2).

During the second half of the twentieth century when dependence on pharmaceutical drugs became the medical norm, our spiritual and emotional health was given less consideration, Only in the last twenty years has there been an academic resurgence in the study of the connection between mind and body. While currently, during the pandemic, our focus has been constantly drawn to the physical acts of social distancing and hand sanitising, recent studies are alerting us to the mental health aspects of ongoing uncertainty and isolation.

In order to stay healthy in body and mind, we cannot ignore the integration of a spiritual dimension. In this book the essays, extracts and poems about healing in its fullest sense are designed to provide a balance between the mental and physical aspects of our lives.

Paul Kraus

Thomas Merton – new seeds of spiritual direction and growth

Merton's parents settled in France where he was born in 1915. His father was a New Zealand artist and his mother was a Quaker. Merton's early life was spent in France and he later moved to England. At one point, he studied briefly at Cambridge University and, after one year, moved to settle in America in 1939 when he felt a calling to become a priest. He entered the Trappist monastery of Gethsemani in Kentucky in December, 1941.

Thomas Merton became a writer, theologian, mystic, scholar and social activist whose life and work has become well known throughout the world-wide church. His life was short and he died tragically in an accident in Thailand at the age of fifty-three in 1968.

Merton contributed significantly to the work of meditation, contemplative prayer and Christian social activism. His book, *Spiritual Direction and Meditation* was radical in the way it spelt out how Christian meditation was a 'new' way of finding intimacy with God. Through this book, he encouraged his readers to renew the practice of meditation and contemplative prayer.

He presented to the church a different way of following Christ. His influence on meditation and contemplative prayer has stayed with us. Within the time he was a hermit, he wrote a superb autobiography called *The Seven Storey Mountain*, published in 1948 and becoming a best seller. He also wrote extensively about the mindset of Christian mystics of an earlier age.

Merton's beliefs about the mystery of God's ways in relation to our daily life has a depth and broad universality. He praised the way God works in the lives of people. He emphasised the simplicity and the importance of meditation and the need for us to be released and being let go from this world. He exhorted us to love one another at a deeper level, as God loves us.

The following poem was written not long before he died. It had a strong impact not merely on the Christian world, but in the realm of other religious beliefs as well. Here he expresses his belief in finding what brings serenity and peace to each of us. It incorporates a sense of peace that can be found in times such as the present. This poem also speaks to our own disoriented time.

The following poem expresses his belief in finding what brings serenity and peace to each of us. It incorporates a sense of peace that can be found in times such as the present.

When in the soul of a serene disciple
Thomas Merton

When in the soul of the serene disciple
With no more Fathers to imitate
Poverty is a success,
It is a small thing to say the roof is gone:
He has not even a house.

Stars, as well as friends,
Are angry with the noble ruin.
Saints depart in several directions.

Be still:
There is no longer any need of comment.
It was a lucky wind
That blew away his halo with his cares,
A lucky sea that drowned his reputation.

Here you will find
Neither a proverb nor a memorandum.
There are no ways,
No methods to admire
Where poverty is no achievement.
His God lives in his emptiness like an affliction.

What choice remains?
Well, to be ordinary is not a choice:
It is the usual freedom
Of men without visions.

The 'serene disciple' has no ego to protect, few worries, no anxieties. Rather, they live with an inner peace in an isolation which may be ironical to our age and grants them satisfaction. Isolation might bring with it disadvantages, yet we are no longer bound by the rules of this world. God dwells within each of us, even when we are at a low ebb. The final verse asks an important question about our choices in life. The answer is '...to be ordinary...' to be people without visions, especially of grandness and high achievement. The simplicity of being a 'serene disciple' is a sure answer to our striving. Merton believes we can always become free by our selflessness, by our love of God, who lives within.

(The poem is taken from *Allies On The Journey website*.)

Paul Kraus

Peace and joy in the midst of uncertainty

Peace, perfect peace, in this dark world of sin?
The Blood of Jesus whispers peace within.

Peace, perfect peace, by thronging duties pressed?
To do the will of Jesus, this is rest.

Peace, perfect peace, with sorrows surging round?
On Jesus' bosom nought but calm is found.

Peace, perfect peace, with loved ones far away?
In Jesus' keeping we are safe and they.

Peace, perfect peace, our future all unknown?
Jesus we know, and he is on the throne.

Peace, perfect peace, death shadowing us and ours?
Jesus has vanquished death and all its powers.

Peace, perfect peace: earth's struggles soon shall cease,
And Jesus call us to heaven's perfect peace.

This hymn is taken from an Anglican liturgical resource, *The Book of Common Praise* (With Supplement) used in the Church of England in Australia in the post Second World War era. The words of this hymn, written in nineteenth century England by

Edward Henry Bickersteth (1825-1906), have a contemporary meaning in our twenty-first century. The questions that begin each verse applies to everyone in equal measure. The answers point to the fact that only the spirit and presence of Jesus can grant us peace.

Love alone overcomes fear

Richard Rohr, a Franciscan priest for over fifty years, has for decades been known throughout the church as a teacher, a well-known writer of numerous books that focus on Christian spirituality, as well as healing in its fullest sense. His writing is, to some degree, empowered by his mystical way of thinking about how we live.

His writing is also illustrated by a deep knowledge of the saints throughout the history of the Church. His love for the lifestyle of Francis of Assisi and the framework in which Francis lived has also been a formative influence. As a writer about spirituality and as the founder of the Centre for Action and Contemplation in Alburquerque, New Mexico, his many lectures and his teaching have given him an influence in the church worldwide, as well as in the secular world.

Each of his books focuses on an important aspect of our spirituality, especially about the numerous ways we suffer in one form or another. He has written over twenty books, some of which became best sellers. Each spell out one of life's difficulties or challenges and he explored deep questions of identity, spirituality and meaning. He also explains what he has described as 'the first half' and the 'second half' of our life. His substantial work sits alongside fellow progressive twentieth century writers and philosophers within the Church such as Henri Nouwen and Thomas Merton.

Richard Rohr has lived in the New Mexico province for many years. The Covid virus brought suffering and tragedy across most nations, although its severity has been greatest in Europe, the United States and Brazil. The economic and social disruption it has created has been enormous. This era of illness has, as it were, required us to think again of the re-arrangement of social and economic priorities. It has also prompted a change to our religious priorities. The matter of having our church doors closed, even in Australia for only a relatively short time, and having a limited access to the sacraments, has shaken our mindset.

Rohr has also stated that we need to rearrange our church 'in loving places', to re-prioritise our evangelistic agenda, especially those for whom God is on the outer edge: the poor, the homeless and those who lead lonely lives. In other words, to those people who have little peace or balance; or who experience social justice in this world that grants priority to the wealthy.

We also need to implement policies, in both the world and the church, that give people true hope and not allow us to succumb to the 'organised deceit' of the mass media. Rohr emphasises, especially in this time of the Covid pandemic that the church must be attuned to the great truths of the meaning of Easter. In other words, it needs to bring new life and hope, a resurrection faith to what he called 'short-run' people those who, within society, are the least heard and those who have, at best, a 'second chance' of succeeding.

Rohr acts in what he believes is a truly Franciscan, selfless, 'unorthodox' and generous response. In one sense, his motto is having a pure heart and a singleness of focus. His books all seem to have, in one way or another, the theme that God liberates and loves us. He actually states in his book, *The Universal Christ*: 'We may feel we know who Jesus was, but was he Christ?' Jesus was the loving, liberating and life-giving expression and presence of God.

In his words about the Covid pandemic, Richard Rohr embraces the true meaning of Scripture and tradition, especially his mystical interpretation that we give meaning to this 'box of a disordered world'. He has stated that because we live in an apocalyptic world, we also need to confront the reality of asking what will our new world become. How will attitudes be different in a world with a new 'set of rules'? Self-aggrandisement will no longer rule our earth. This cataclysmic event is an encouragement to work in the spirit of Jesus as Christ.

We live in the paradox of living alone, yet being 'utterly connected'. in quite a different way to what historically happened in the world-wide pandemic of the Spanish flu, one hundred years ago. Rohr poignantly asks: where is the presence of Christ in the world of Covid-19? He also states, in relation to the three days between Good Friday and the great celebration of Easter Day, that we, as Christians, should embrace the presence of Christ in our lives.

Rohr spoke to his fellow Americans, asking them to put aside issues such as race and poverty in the awareness that those who belong to these categories have a much greater chance of succumbing to the ravages of this virus.

Richard Rohr practises and teaches his 'Franciscan alternative orthodoxy' in his Centre for Action and Contemplation (CAC) in Albuquerque, New Mexico. This centre also teaches online and is received by countless people throughout the world. By this means, as well as his messages of redemption and love in his twenty books, Rohr recognises that Christ lives in us, grants us true wholeness.

In his books, Rohr repeatedly explores questions of identity, spirituality and meaning. He has written about transcendence and 'endless horizons' in relation to the smallness of our ego with its endless preoccupations and our seeking for a 'deeper truth'. He has always endorsed meditation and contemplative prayer as means of bringing us into life's true perspective.

Paul Kraus

Returning to the heart

For many, Covid-19 has unexpectedly begun a spiritual awakening and a re-evaluation of life's values. The tsunami of a tiny virus shut down factories, financial institutions, offices, places of worship, planes and trains, schools and universities, overwhelmed healthcare and exposed the flaws of the people and institutions that govern us. But didn't the internet flourish! We newly discovered its human, spiritual potential. It allowed us to volunteer, in great numbers, to help others, to express solidarity with the worst affected, to meet and pray, to accompany the lonely, to discuss what all this craziness might mean for the future.

The crisis has exposed fundamental flaws in our view of the world, our environment and social structures. We are all in the same storm, rich and poor, north and south. But we are clearly not in the same boat. There is a zip code and racial factor in how the virus strikes. So what does 'getting back to normal' mean? Do we want to go back, or, alternatively, to learn from new sources of wisdom how to change, to be converted in heart and remember what we forgot, even that we had lost when we were burning the candle at both ends?

In the black comedy *In Bruges*, two hit men – friends as much as killers can be – are forced to go under cover. One has been commissioned to kill the other who is secretly suicidal. One morning, as he is sitting on a park bench, the assassin joins him to shoot him. But he sees with horror that his friend is preparing to shoot himself. Forgetting his commission, he prevents him. This act of natural goodness restores a real human value and the story ends with dark but true meanings. The world has been on a course of self-destruction. Has the virus, a deadly assassin, become a friend saving us? Enemies can be our best spiritual friends.

Laurence Freeman OSB

From a letter in *Meditato*, Newsletter of the World Community for Christian Meditation, August 2020.

(*Used with the permission of Fr Laurence Freeman.*)

A prayer for healing

Almighty and all-merciful God,
lover of the human race, healer of all our wounds,
in whom there is no shadow of death,
save us in this time of crisis;
grant wisdom and courage to our leaders;
watch over all medical people
as they tend the sick and work for a cure;
stir in us a sense of solidarity beyond all isolation;
if our doors are closed, let our hearts be open.

By the power of your love, destroy the virus of fear,
hope that may never die
and the light of Easter, the triumph of life,
may shine upon us and the whole world.

Through Jesus Christ, the Lord risen from the dead,
who lives and reigns for ever and ever.
Amen.

Mark Coleridge

(Mark Coleridge is Archbishop of Brisbane.)

A time for regeneration

This April, when Jews and Christians around the globe retold the Passover story as we do each year, the Exodus account of the ten plagues of Egypt no longer seemed a distant Bronze Age myth. To-day's plague may not be as deadly as those visited on Pharaoh, but it's lethal enough. A friend who works in a nearby senior home here in upstate New York tells a now familiar of exhausted nurses, inadequate supples, and daily deaths. We are keenly aware of the devastation among our neighbours in New York City, and fear what will happen as the virus spreads in other urban areas, through prisons, and in poorer countries lacking the same healthcare resources and infrastructure. Meanwhile, mass layoffs and failing businesses around the world threaten a bitter aftermath of economic desperation and stunted hopes.

Whether or not this plague, like the biblical ones, is a punishment, it certainly is apocalyptic. I don't mean this in an end-of-the-world way, but rather in the literal sense of apocalypse as an unveiling a revelation of how things really are. This crisis has ripped the cover of certain truths about our souls and our society. Some of these truths are ugly. We see exposed the reality of public corruption; murderous inequalities in the provision of healthcare; or for that matter, our societies unnatural choice to warehouse so many of its grandparents in underfunded institutions where they live and die in isolation, even when no pandemic rages.

But the crisis has revealed other truths, too. It has called forth countless acts of solidarity and compassion, each one proof of the divine spark in humankind. It has cast light on the sacrificial efforts of nurses, doctors, police officers, delivery drivers and grocery clerks. It has shown that millions of our fellow human beings, of all creeds and walks of life, will jump at a chance to be their brothers' and sisters' keeper, if only by grieving with the grieving or wearing a face mask.

In a time of crisis whether a pandemic, a terrorist attack or a war people are quick to say that 'things will never be the same'. This comes from an understandable urge. Faced with suffering of such magnitude, our instinct is to find meaning in it by claiming it has shifted the course of history. In reality, while some things may change in the wake of the pandemic, most will not. This crisis reveals many truths, but in itself will not transform or heal or renew.

Christians should not be surprised or discouraged by this. We expect regeneration from another source. For us, the decisive turning point was not in 2020, or 9/11, or 1945, or 1776, but as Stanley Hauerwas (a theologian) likes to remind us – in AD 33, when Jesus, who had been killed, rose again in the flesh, alive from the dead. The only way to face mass death honestly without despairing is to believe that resurrection is real, that death will not have the last word.

'God hath made no decree to distinguish the seasons of his mercies', wrote John Donne. 'He can bring thy summer out of winter, though thou have no spring; though in the ways of fortune, or understanding, or conscience, thou have been benighted till now, wintered and frozen, moulded and eclipsed, damped and benumbed, smothered and stupefied till now, now God comes to thee, not as in the dawning of the day, not as in the bud of the spring, but as the sun at noon, to illustrate all shadows, as the sheaves in harvest, to fill all penuries. All occasions invite his mercies, and all times are his seasons.'

This time, too, is his season. It's up to us to help break the ground; he will renew the world.

Peter Mommsen,Editor,
Plough Quarterly Magazine,
New York.
20 April 2020.
(*Used with the permission of the editor.*)

A better way is possible

A rising tide of populist nationalism. Polarised debates that leave people in a permanent state of confrontation. A global pandemic which has exposed the weakness of free markets. Ideologies and hatred being spread on social media.

As Pope Francis writes in his new encyclical letter, the world 'shows signs of a certain regression'.

Fratelli Tutti is the 83-year-old Roman pontiff's attempt to show that a better way is possible. Covid-19 has shown that we are 'a global community, all win the same boat'. The Pope calls for a new kind of politics, one that is kinder and more tender, open to dialogue and expressing love of neighbour.

To adapt the popular prayer attributed to St Francis: 'where there is populism', Pope Francis focuses on people: where there is nationalism, he calls for reform of the United Nations; where there is individualism, he pushes for solidarity; where there is digital trolling, he asks for kindness; where there is inequality, he urges fairer distribution; when politicians hate, he recommends dialogue; when there is ideology, he calls for genuine faith.

The encyclical takes an uncompromising stand against the 'myopic, extremist, resentful and aggressive nationalism' that Francis sees across Europe, the United States and parts of Latin America. One official in Rome put it to me this way: 'It's a kick in the head to the rising tide of barbarism'.

The Encyclical is the third major document of Francis' pontificate. The first, *Evangelii Gaudium*, an apostolic constitution, offers a manifesto for church renewal. The second, *Laudato Si'* (extracts from which are at the beginning of this book), an encyclical, recasts the church's teaching on protecting the natural world. And his third, *Fratelli Tutti*, is a natural next step, as it looks to repair and enrich relationships across the human family. There are three points that stand out when reading the encyclical.

First, it shows that at the heart of the pontificate of Pope Francis is a Gospel-based leadership rooted in the spirit of St Francis of Assisi, the Pope's namesake. In *Fratelli Tutti*, the Pope approaches the complexities of global politics with the story of the Good Samaritan and the story of the 1219 peace mission, where Francis of Assisi crossed the battle lines of the Crusades, to meet the Sultan of Egypt in a bid to end the conflict,

Both stories emphasise crossing the existential borders that separate people. St Francis, the Pope writes, had an 'openness of heart, which knew no bounds and transcended differences of origin, nationality, colour or religion'. Francis' reflections on the contemporary political situation and his warnings about nationalism and populism are an attempt to apply the Gospel in the spirit of the poor man from Assisi.

The parable of the Good Samaritan, Francis points out, is not 'abstract moralising, nor is its message merely social and ethical' but shows how humanity can be changed by coming into contact with suffering. Francis' vision is non-ideological, and its power is in its simplicity. In *Fratelli Tutti*, he critiques both ends of the political spectrum the free market will not resolve the world's problems nor will liberal approaches which don't offer a 'shared narrative' and ignore 'human weakness', Instead, he focuses on practical actions which, step by step, build the Kingdom of God. Far from rejecting the work of politicians, he praises politics as an attempt to put charity into action. 'While one person can help another by providing something to eat, the politician creates a job', the Pope writes.

Here we come to the second point, which is how Francis' encyclical sits within the Catholic Social Teaching tradition and seeks to apply it to a contemporary context.

One development of the tradition can be founding the Pope's reflection on the centuries-old Just War teaching, which sets the conditions that would make armed conflict morally justifiable. Although he stops just short of abolishing the theory altogether, he write only of the 'potential right' to go to war and warns that the development of nuclear and chemical weapons means they have an 'uncontrollable destructive power over great numbers of innocent civilians'.

One of the conditions of a Just War is that, even when going to war is morally justified, only proportionate force is used. 'In recent decades, every single war has been ostensibly 'justified', Francis explains. 'It is very difficult nowadays to invoke the rational criteria elaborated in earlier centuries to speak of the possibility of a "just war". Never again war!' Francis is pushing the church a step closer to a complete rejection of war, a year after his visit to Japan when he declared that the possession and not just the use of nuclear weapons was immoral.

Fratelli Tutti is the first papal encyclical to offer a detailed critique of digital culture. The Pope warns that 'social aggression has found unparalleled room for expansion through computers and mobile devices' and that ideologies have been given 'free rein'. Social media, he says, has seen 'some political figures' say things in the 'crudest of terms' which in the past would have risked the loss of universal respect. If the message of *Laudato Si'* is 'Everything is connected', the message of *Fratelli Tutti* is 'Everyone is connected'.

Christopher Lamb

(*Permission has been given by the author to use this extract from the article 'A better way is possible'* **The Tablet,** *10 October 2020.*)

A holy moment

When striving ceases, when ego dies,
When only praise and alleluias rise,
When I awake on Resurrection's morn,
When I shall glimpse that glorious dawn.

Then shall I see my Master's face
And stand in his amazing grace.
Unceasing love forever free,
It is this Lord who died for me.

A holy moment that will be,
Sheer ecstasy to be set free
From tyranny of self; from fear
And doubt, anxiety ever near.

A holy moment that will be
To meet the angels and to see
Loved ones from this veil of tears,
There to dwell beyond all years.

No more hunger, no more thirst,
Then the last shall be the first,
When this puzzling tapestry,
Profound in its eternity I see.

A holy moment that will be!

Paul Kraus

A holy moment

In one way, the Covid pandemic is almost a parable about the precariousness of our lives. In the realm of universal truth, all of us are born, live and eventually die. I wrote this poem after I had been informed that I did not have long to live, following my initial cancer diagnosis.

The everlasting mercy

O Christ who holds the open gate,
O Christ who drives the furrow straight,
O Christ, the plough, O Christ, the laughter
Of holy white birds flying after,
Lo, all my heart's field red and torn,
And Thou wilt bring the young green corn
The young green corn forever singing;
And when the field is fresh and fair
Thy blessed feet shall glitter there,
And we will walk the weeded field,
And tell the golden harvest's yield,
The corn that makes the holy bread
By which the soul of man is fed,
The holy bread, the food unpriced,
Thy everlasting mercy, Christ.

John Masefield

This is a brief extract from a long narrative poem by the famous English poet John Masefield (1878-1967) who achieved the distinction of becoming the Poet Laureate of Britain from 1930 to 1967. The theme of this long poem is redemption. It is about a hero whose spiritual emptiness leads to failure and suffering. The hero himself is spiritually saved by God's great love. He has a special moment, an epiphany which leads to redemption and rebirth. Redemption, grace, spiritual rebirth, as well as weakness and ultimate salvation also form the main ideas of a number of poems and articles throughout these pages.

About the author

Paul Kraus was born in Austria in October 1944. He came to Australia with his parents, who were Post-War immigrants in late 1949. The family settled in Sydney and it was in that city that he spent most of his life. He studied at school and at the Conservatorium of Music. He was a mature age student, one of the foundation undergraduate students at Macquarie University, from where he graduated in early 1970 with a B.A. He later completed postgraduate degrees in Modern History, English Language and Literature and the Philosophy of Education at the University of Sydney. His career meandered between senior high school teaching in Catholic schools, writing educational textbooks, becoming a poet and working as an editor.

At the age of fifty-two, he was diagnosed with the life-threatening cancer mesothelioma. With great self-discipline in the realm of nutrition and various healing modalities, including prayer and meditation, he eventually survived that illness and overturned the medical prognosis that his remaining journey on this earth would be rather short. Since recovering from mesothelioma he been treated for a heart problem and has suffered from metastatic prostate cancer. He has also had surgery to remove a large brain tumour which, to his gratitude, was benign.

In recent years he has written a number of books and has written poetry. He leads a meditation group at a St Benedict Parish in Brisbane. Since being diagnosed with cancer, his life has been transformed by the power, wonder and discipline of a contemplative life. He believes that poetry is an expression of the soul, 'saying the unsayable'. He has found creativity an important means that grants him faith, hope and love. In one sense, he regards the writing of poetry akin to being in a state of prayer. In an independent, yet in an allied way, he finds that receiving the sacrament in the Eucharist is another means of love and grace. It is regenerating, granting the real, inexpressible gift of Jesus himself.

Acknowledgments

In gratitude, the author acknowledges the following contributors whose writing contributes to this book.

Mere Christianity by C.S.lewis@copyrightCSLewisPte.Ltd, 1942,1943.1944,1952. Professor Tomáš Halík for permission to reproduce his essay, *The Pandemic And Theology* from *Durham Martyrs Parish Magazine*, Durham City, England. *Learning from COVID-19 that we are not alone, but there is much separation*, published in Global Sisters Report, used with the permission of Gail De George, Editor of *Global Sisters Report*, 25 May 2020; Leah Libresco-Sargeant, *Comment Journal*, 4 June 2020 for allowing her essay *Locating Our Invisible Wounds* to be reproduced; Lynn Ungar, poet and writer, California for permission to reproduce her poem *Pandemic*, March, 2020. A.B.C. National Radio for the use of *This An Apocalypse? We Certainly Hope So - You Should Too*, by Catherine Keller and John Thatamanil, 20 April 2020; *The New York Times*, 22 March 2020 for permission to reproduce *Where Is God In A Pandemic?* James Martin, S.J. *Litany of Solidarity And Hope During A Pandemic*, jesuitsource.org by Joseph P. Shadle, Xavier University, Ohio; *A Prayer For Our Uncertain Times*, Rev. Dr William Barber, Collected poems on COVID crisis, jesuitsource.org. Professor Sam Ben Meir, Mercy College, New York City, for permission to reproduce his essay, *The Theology of Pandemics*; Gerard O'Connell, for permission to use his article '*Pope Francis shares his vision for civil aftermath*' from *America the Jesuit Review* 17 April 2020; Joseph Capizzi, '*What am I to say? Breaking Ground,*

24 June 2020; *And our hearts are restless till they find their rest in you*, Nicholas Shield, District Deputy for Washington, D.C. Knights Commander of Columbus; *The Wisdom Of The Classics*, Shambalha Press, 1994, by Thomas Merton for reproducing his poem *When in the soul of a serene disciple*, *The Book Of Common Praise*, (Australia) for the hymn, *Peace, Perfect Peace*; Fr. Richard Leonard, S.J and *The Tablet*, for *God does not send us plagues to teach us things*... Fr. Robert Imbelli for permission to reproduce his essay, *Jesuit Karl Rahner, on what it means to love Jesus*. America Media, 11 October 2020. Christopher Lamb and *The Tablet* for permission to reproduce extracts from *A better way is possible*. The editor of *America, the Jesuit Review* for permission to reproduce the essay, *What can St. Augustine teach us about living through a pandemic?* by Kathleen Bonnette, May 28, 2020.

October 2020

www.ingramcontent.com/pod-product-compliance
Lightning Source LLC
Chambersburg PA
CBHW010707020526
44107CB00082B/2701